Marketing is Dead.
Long Live Purposing.

*How to connect with your customers
in the new, intuitive way.*

First Edition.
© Justin JG Cooper 2017

"As you search for your true self, you are peeling back the layers of an onion."

Bill George.

"...nobody can stand truth if it is told to him. Truth can be tolerated only if you discover it yourself because then, the pride of discovery makes the truth palatable."

Fritz Perls.

"Be yourself, everyone else is already taken."

as Oscar Wilde never said.

CONTENT:

Chapter 1
The Illusion

Chantelle was hot – *smoking hot.* Ken was a God. Together they were mesmerising.

They should have been models, but on the day they were due to be selected, the talent scouts were off duty. They *knew* they were hot, but we didn't care. We were all smitten.

Chantelle moved like a panther – turning the carpet between the entrance of our open-plan office and the boardroom into a catwalk. Her blouse was always shy of a few too many buttons at the top. Her dress was too tight for modesty, her legs too shapely, and her lips far too red for comfort.

Ken strutted down the corridor like he owned the building. His shirt was two sizes too small, and it highlighted his bulging biceps and chiselled chest. His shoulders would have made Arnold Schwarzenegger weep.

Chantelle and Ken had one job, and one job only: to keep the men and women in our department completely focussed on their assets, and not on the agency's dodgy concept boards.

Welcome to my first marketing department. It is 1988.

Sex sold our ad agency's concepts way before the creative team had popped its first pills of the day. Chantelle and Ken were the agency's key weapons to ensure us poor brand managers couldn't focus on anything but their *gluteus maximi.*

Marketing in the Eighties, Nineties, and Noughties was founded on and driven by image. It was a game in which we made our brands as sexy as possible to entice consumers away from the competition. It was a sophisticated tool to create an illusion for the consumer. As long as there were smoke and mirrors involved, you could get the consumer to buy just about anything.

I know because I was part of this system myself. I have been as guilty as the next marketer of 'gilding the lily' to convince consumers that some ingredient in minute quantities could change their lives. In my case it was to claim that protein could transform the shine and lustre of a woman's hair. I remember badgering the Operations Manager into allowing me to claim that ingredient X would add protein to someone's hair. This prompted him to exclaim in a strong Dutch accent: 'If I spat in this 20,000 litre tank, there would still be more protein than if we added that ingredient!"

Bless him, he didn't wear the same star-spangled glasses we in the Marketing Department did. He was a realist. We were dream-weavers. And never the twain shall meet.

Then everything changed. After 15 years of working in packaged goods marketing and 10 years of working in small business marketing, I had an epiphany.

Suddenly I just wasn't comfortable with the fact that my industry was founded on 'mind control,' half-truths and deceit. I just didn't want to be a part of that world anymore. It felt wrong. I wanted to tell the truth about what I was doing. And the more I thought about it, the more I decided that the truth was more interesting than the lie.

And at the same time I was reaching this conclusion, consumers were too. The world was changing, and I wanted to change with it.

That's why I have written this book – to show you how to replace image and spin for truth and Purpose. I want to show you how to stop 'playing the game' at work and in business, and how to start playing your *own* game. I want to show you how you can stop going through the motions of being successful, and reclaim who you really are – to be yourself. Because by doing so you will become happier, more fulfilled, more effective, and ultimately more successful.

I want to show you how you can replace 'selling' with 'helping,' by establishing a Purposeful dialogue with your like-minded tribe.

This book is designed for anyone looking for greater clarity on who they are and what they stand for. It's for anyone confused about what makes them, their business, or their brand unique. And it's for those feeling a little confused about where they are going right now. It's also designed for anyone who is questioning the way things are currently being done, and is open to considering a new way.

It's a new take on old marketing, by an old marketer. It's a collection of ideas to build a case for working and doing business in a new way. It's a practical book that will show you how to connect who you are with how you work, in order to create a unique and authentic offer for your customers. In the coming pages I explain why I believe that Purpose is essential to being successful and fulfilled in business, and I provide a framework for how to articulate that Purpose in a way that allows your customers and/or employers to completely 'get' and trust you, and/or your business, and brand.

I'll show you a new technique called *Business Visualisations,* which allows you to explore your subconscious and to understand your *why*, in a far more powerful way than when using rational thought. These visualisations are a type of guided meditation, and in chapters 4, 7, 8 and 9 you'll have the opportunity to download and play these visualisations on your smartphone or computer.

Meditation has long been recognised as an excellent tool to help relax, de-stress, and unlock people's creativity. However, its use as a tool for business is a new concept. In fact, when I first launched my online course in late 2012 justinjgcooper.com/your-authentic-business-details, I believe it was the only business course using meditation as its foundation.

I hope there will be a time in the not-too-distant future when meditation, and other forms of mindfulness, will become standard practice in business. Why? Because rational thought, when used in isolation, is limiting in its capacity to generate original and creative ideas. To be truly happy, productive, and successful in business means combining our rational, intuitive, and emotional thinking – to create a 'whole brain' approach. You will read more about this in Chapter 10.

By the end of this book you should have a good idea of what drives you and what makes you unique. You will have a much clearer idea of who your ideal customer is, how you can make a real difference to them through the work you do, and/or the products and services you sell. You will also have the opportunity in the final chapter to create a Vision for where you want your work, business, or brand to take you, along with some ideas on how you might be able to get there.

If you don't believe in the power of the imagination, then it's best to stop reading now, as the ideas here will seem too fantastic and fanciful for you to take seriously. But if you are open to learning and trying something new, then welcome aboard...

Chapter 2
Marketing is Dead?

At 12.35pm on 17th December 2004 traditional marketing died peacefully in its sleep. No one turned up to the funeral because they didn't realise it had passed away. Even today most people believe it's still alive, presumably living on the moon with Elvis Presley and JFK.

What prompted this untimely death?

On that day the one-millionth user signed up to Facebook, and the rules of marketing changed forever. The power shifted from the company to the consumer.

All of a sudden consumers took control of how products and services were perceived. The 'mind control' previously exerted by companies through advertising was waning. Consumers now had an inbuilt 'BS-ometre' that told them when they were hearing porky pies. The clever marketing campaigns built on half-truths and spin didn't seem to be working quite so well.

Fake it till you make it

Back in the early 90's we used to regularly 'make stuff up' in order to sell products. And we generally got away with it, as long as it had a good image, a unique and relevant positioning, was supported by a wonder ingredient, and had a decent marketing budget. I was working in London for a hair-care company; my second FMCG company (fast moving consumer goods), liaising with our US Head Office to launch a new brand. At the time, in the early 1990s, the US was seriously into the 'big hair look,' but the UK wasn't. That 'just walked out of a poodle parlour' thing wasn't quite cutting it in London any more. But the US wanted a global brand for this new product, and we were instructed to prepare for launch in the UK. We argued strongly against launch, saying the positioning they had developed would have less appeal than toilet paper with finger holes through it. Our concerns were heard, and the compromise was that we were allowed to market test the concept in the UK.

However the extra time this added meant that we had to launch the concept to our sales team the day after the results came in from research. The concept bombed. As saying 'I told you so' to our sales team wasn't particularly helpful, we decided on a different tack. We would invent our own concept. So I sat long into the night, staring at my computer screen, searching for an idea. At around 11pm (and 5 cups of coffee later) I had had my 'a-ha' moment, and a new concept was born out of thin air. The following day we announced that we wouldn't be running with the US concept, but a new one, founded on common sense and consumer demand. "No problem" was the response, "as long as we still have a good marketing budget to support it, it'll work." In the end the US launch was canned, and we were no longer required to launch our refined take on their 'big hair' concept.

The point is, we were in the business of making up the USP (Unique Selling Proposition) on the fly, and it didn't matter, because as long as the packaging design, advertising, promotion, and pricing was right, the consumer would buy it.

The Authentic Revolution

But 10 years later things had changed. Consumers were no longer prepared to buy something just because it contained a wonder ingredient, had a sexy image, a competitive price, and a great ad campaign behind it. With the growth of the internet and social media, armies of customers started chatting openly to one another about what they thought of the products and services they had tried. This was nothing short of a revolution. The ability companies had in controlling their customers' perceptions of their brands had diminished significantly. The power shifted from the company to the consumer. Rather than being *told* what to think about a product, consumers formed their own opinion, then shared that opinion with other consumers. It was the end of old-fashioned marketing as we knew it.

This new dawn started tentatively with user groups and discussion boards, but over the years has flourished into whole communities. In desperation, some large brand companies tried to regulate this discussion through their own social media sites, but this tended to backfire. Consumers started questioning the claims and promises made in advertising, preferring to trust reviews and comments made by other consumers. The number of Facebook users has now eclipsed one billion people, cementing the shift from the company to the consumer. And of course the myriad of other social media sites makes this shift all the more permanent.

Walking hand-in-hand with this online revolution is a shift in consumer psyche. Consumers are spoilt for choice, so they are harder to please. To compound matters (for traditional marketers) they are getting tired of accumulating more and more 'bling.' Instead of more 'stuff,' consumers are looking for products that feel genuine and experiential. Bombarded with excessive information, they have become marketing-savvy, and weary of image and spin. They are over 'fake' - it's *so* last century. All that smoke and mirrors simply doesn't cut it for them. Now they're looking for **authenticity** – they want people, brands and companies to tell it straight. They want to know what they stand for, what drives them, and how their products and services will actually help them. It's far more engaging, credible, and sustainable.

In short, they want products and services that are **authentic and genuine**. People crave it, and they are choosing authentic over fake. That's because if something feels authentic, you can trust it. Trust has always been essential to the buying process, but now it is more important than ever. We've moved from loving image to loving substance. People are asking deeper questions about the products and services they buy. Traditional marketing simply isn't geared up to answer those questions. The trouble is that most businesses, marketing, and advertising agencies are still using traditional marketing techniques. But in doing so, they are losing their customers' trust.

How authentic is *your* business, brand or career?

Here's a simple exercise to get you thinking:

justinjgcooper.com/blog/how-authentic-is-your-business

The Power of 'Why'

Simon Sinek wrote a very powerful book called *'Start with Why,'* in which he proposed that successful leaders and businesses had one thing in common – they were all clear about and could easily explain why they were doing what they did. Then they went about instilling this *why* into the product, service or idea they offered, the people they worked with, and the audience they served. As a result, everyone became more inspired and motivated to work with or buy the concept. Here's a 5-minute clip of Simon Sinek explaining the core idea during his inspirational 2009 TED talk:
https://youtu.be/IPYeCltXpxw

The consumer is asking **why** of the people they buy from: Why are you doing this? Why did you decide to produce your widgets in Bangladesh, in a factory that has no health and safety requirements? Why did you decide to launch this business? What is your Vision for your business? Very few people were interested in this kind of questioning in the past, but they are now.

I love Simon's work, but I would change one word. I would swap **why** for **you**. I'd like people to **Start**

with You. That's because we can't explain our **why** rationally. It's impossible to do. The rational brain is only geared up to answer two questions: 'what?' and 'how?' It's easy to consider the questions 'what shall I do today?' and 'how will I do it?' But when trying to answer the question *why* – as in 'why am I really doing this work?' – the rational brain goes blank, and the answers we get back are superficial, artificial, and borrowed from others. We don't *mean* to dodge the question, it's just that our rational brains can't process it.

'Why' is Hidden

For many years, as a marketing consultant, I tried asking my clients *why*. Despite becoming adept at asking the same question in 50 different ways, the outcome was always the same. People would always struggle. They either gave me the answer they thought they *should* give, or an answer that someone they respected would give. Which explains why 'honesty and integrity' kept popping up all the time. It used to drive me nuts. I would write down the 10 most common answers, and tick them off as the client gave them to me. I felt like shouting 'Bingo!' once they'd ticked off all 10.

I started reading up on the human brain, to understand how it works, or rather, what we currently understand about how it works (which isn't much from what I can glean). I discovered that the current thinking is that our beliefs and values are predominately stored in the limbic brain, and that you can't access this when you are in a rational state. I also discovered that people need to be in a relaxed state of mind in order to detach from rational thinking, and that being relaxed and not stressing about the question is actually the key to being able to start answering the question *why.* The trouble is, when you are being asked questions about your business, in a business setting, the last thing you are is relaxed and detached. In business settings people tend to be attentive and focussed. At this point you can only give rational responses. The conclusion I have made is that *why* can only be answered when you are relaxed enough to tap into your emotional and intuitive self. And that is not a state of mind people tend to turn up with at work each morning. I'll talk more about how I discovered a way to solve this problem in Chapter 6.

But for now let me say this: I believe it is essential for us to spend time understanding *ourselves* (as individuals, teams, and/or businesses) in terms of why we do the work we do, and what we are here to do for our customers, before we spend another dollar on marketing and promoting ourselves. This will give us the tools to explain what we offer in a far more authentic and unique way, thus building trust and credibility with our potential customers from the outset.

Simon Sinek has stated that it is not the shareholder *or* the customer who is the most important person to the success of a business. He argues that it is the employees (and business partners) who are the most important art of the equation, because by motivating and inspiring *them*, you ensure your customers are looked after. Happy customers mean higher sales, greater profits, and even happier shareholders. This sentiment is echoed in the brilliant book *Conscious Capitalism,* a must read for anyone interested in the new paradigm of conscious business practice.

Start with You

I would argue that there's someone even *more* important to the success of your business, brand or career. And that person is **you.** The best analogy here is the safety demonstration on an aircraft. The cabin crew always say, "should the cabin experience a sudden loss in pressure, oxygen masks will drop down from above your seat. Place the mask over your mouth and nose." This is followed by the crucial phrase: "If you are travelling with a child or someone who requires assistance, **secure your own mask first, before assisting the other person.**"

The trouble is, most of us forget that bit. We hurl ourselves into the market, looking to make a difference to our clients without first examining what we are really capable of.

As the owner of your business, the custodian of your brand, or the captain of your own career, **you** are the key to success. You are the driving force, the inspiration and *raison d'etre* for your product, service, or career. You are the one driven by a higher Purpose and a Mission to improve the lives of your customers. To ignore that is to miss a fundamental part of the equation. And that's exactly what traditional marketing does. It ignores **you** completely. It doesn't take into account or value why you, your company, or your brand exists – or what you believe in, and what makes you tick. It considers this to be totally irrelevant, because it doesn't fit into its neat, rational, and scientific framework.

Only **you** understand why you are here to do this work, or offer this product or service. You – and only you – know the Purpose behind the work you do, the business you run, or the brand you manage, and how it has the potential to make a huge difference to your customers.

I believe this lack of focus on *you* is a major cause of business failure. In the case of a business or brand, this failure is often down to the fact that the people running the company don't truly believe in what they are selling. They are going through the motions, but their hearts aren't quite in it. They don't have a clearly-defined company Purpose or client Mission, which means they don't give their all. They are doing it for the money, not the love; and eventually it shows.

The key to overcoming this situation is for individuals, businesses and brands to get clear on their Purpose, then express it as a customer Mission that explains how you will solve a genuine client problem.

While revenue and profit are essential to survival in the short to medium term, we need to be inspired and motivated by what we are doing to thrive in the long term. We need to believe that what we are doing will make a difference. All the other ingredients for success might be there: good idea, good product, good service, and a fair price. But where's the desire? Where's the conviction? Is there a direct connection between what we stand for and what we offer? Are we working with like-minded business partners and customers? Do we feel motivated and inspired to go to work?

In today's climate, if these elements are missing, our businesses are destined to fail in the long term. If there's a disconnect between what we believe in and what we are doing, we struggle. In the past this didn't necessarily matter – we just got on with the job in hand. But something fundamental has changed. Today we **need** that spark of excitement, that sense of higher Purpose. That's what gives us the drive to try harder, the imagination to come up with better ideas, and the confidence to try new approaches. Purpose has the power to keep us going in the face of adversity.

Where does this shift in thinking come from?

Most commentators agree that human civilisation has moved from the 'Industrial Age' (roughly 1700-1960) to the 'Information/Digital Age' from the 1960s onwards. Some commentators describe a new era that began in 2012 called the 'Conscious Age.' This has coincided with people searching for more meaning, authenticity, Purpose, and greater human connection in their lives. Sure, there's still plenty of fear, anger, and division in the world, but this is a natural reaction by those who are still clinging to the old way of doing things. We are starting to think and feel differently. Our needs are changing. With it comes a demand for greater connectedness, which is at odds with the way that new technologies (e.g. the Internet and smartphones) have made many people feel disconnected. And this means that people are searching for like-minded 'tribes,' where they can feel heard, supported, and accepted.

In their book Dawn of the Akashic Age (Simon & Schuster 2013), authors Ervin Laszlo and Kingsley Dennis point to a new model of working based on "shared-interest as opposed to self-interest." They herald the new era of cottage industries springing up, with "thousands of people working from home, supplying individualised items direct to clients world-wide, earning personal feedback, and developing direct producer-customer relations."

How could traditional marketing – with its reliance on a centralised system of communications and a target-market approach of categorising consumers into neat silos – possibly work in this new world order?

Chapter 3
Stop Listening to Everyone Else

"If I had asked my customers what they wanted
they would have said a faster horse..."

Attributed to Henry Ford, but no evidence exists
that he actually said it.

Faster Horses

Henry Ford was one smart cookie. He realised that
to be successful he needed to ignore his customers.

He knew there was no point asking them what they wanted, because what he had to offer was so much better.

If he *had* listened to them, he would have had to invent a faster horse. Why? Because that's all they knew – they didn't realise he had a better idea until he told them. That's because it was an idea so big, they couldn't imagine it. And while there's no evidence that Henry ever did actually make that famous statement about 'faster horses', his visionary thinking is clear.

He had a bold Vision for the future, to produce an automobile that cost a fraction of the price of its competitors. He developed a car for the masses at a time when most automobiles were designed and priced exclusively for the super-rich. He designed an assembly line capable of producing cars in mass quantities at very low cost. He imagined (and lobbied for) a network of roads across the USA to carry his new Model T. He dreamed of what could be, rather than accepting what was. He didn't listen to his customers, instead giving them what he knew they needed.

"Not listening – la la la!"

Now obviously I'm not suggesting we should stop listening to our customers when we it comes to *delivering* your products or services to them. That would be ridiculous. You clearly need to move heaven and earth to make their experience with you amazing. You need to ensure they are happy with the whole experience, from start to finish.

I'm talking here about not listening to them when it comes to working out **what you offer** to your customers. I'm saying stop asking them to innovate for you – that's *your* job. They don't know what amazing ideas you have for them, they just want to be wowed by your innovative product or service delivered at a price that justifies the reward.

Expecting your customer to tell you what they want is a trap – they don't know what you're really capable of. They have no idea what is possible beyond their current experience of the category. And besides, as Steve Jobs famously said, "You can't just ask customers what they want and then try to give that to them. By the time you get it built, they'll want something new."

If you run a business, a brand, or are looking for a new career direction, there's only one person who knows what you are truly capable of, and that's you. Your customer hasn't got a clue about the crazy ideas floating around in your head (or your team's heads) about how you could reinvent the market you operate in. If you do ask them what they want, most of the time they'll just play back what they know is currently available — *a horse, just faster.*

But when you give them something they didn't expect — in Ford's case, an affordable car — and that something happens to be just what they needed, then you are playing in a very different field, with the potential for significant success. *Cirque de Soleil* didn't seek to improve the circus experience — they reinvented it. If they had asked their customers what they wanted, the answer might have been 'more acrobats and less lions.' The end result may well have been an improvement on the current circus model, but not the completely new experience that they created with their combination of high-energy theatre performance and skilful acrobatics. In the same way, Elon Musk didn't ask drivers what they wanted, because he already knew he wanted to give them the first ever mass-produced electric plug-in car. He had the

Vision and desire to change the game – and the resources to make it happen. And Uber didn't seek to invent a better taxi service that had more cars available during peak traffic (which is probably what people would have said they wanted). Instead they created an army of private taxis that could be deployed with a touch of a smartphone button, without actually buying any taxis themselves.

There are plenty of other examples of Purpose-driven brand creation (Dyson, Google, Apple and so on), but at this point you might be thinking, 'that's all well and good for *them* – they had huge financial backing to make their ideas happen – I don't!'

In some examples that's true, but in most cases the business owner had to convince investors to stump up money to make their dream come true. It was the power of the idea and its commercial potential that got it going – not the investment money itself.

So the most important thing for the success of your career, business, or brand is to get clear on **why** you are doing what you do. Then you need to articulate how you can change the way things are done in your market, and how you can make a real difference to your customers. You'll have an opportunity to explore this by doing a couple of intuitive visualisation exercises in Chapter 8.

The biggest issue I have with the term 'marketing,' is that it places the emphasis on 'the market,' suggesting that this should be the key focus. This assumes that the market has all the power, and that it can dictate what you do, and what you decide to sell. But as I pointed out in the previous chapter, I believe the real power to make things happen resides with **you** – with your potential to deliver something new, amazing, and genuinely different for your customers. By slavishly asking the market what it wants, we actually do our customers a disservice, by falling into the trap of delivering mediocrity and sameness. But by shifting the focus back to the person with the dream of creating a unique experience, a quantum shift takes place. Instead of thinking about what is, we start thinking in terms of 'what if?' We start to think more imaginatively and innovatively.

Of course, you absolutely should ask your customer how they'd like your new idea delivered. This information can be used to develop a better design and delivery system for your product or service. But it's no good asking your customer to describe a new idea that you haven't imagined yourself yet. That's your job.

Ignore Your Competitors

The other problem with traditional marketing is that it encourages us to obsess about our competitors. We become fixated with the 'faster – higher – stronger' approach. We become fixated with the desire to destroy our competitors. But this approach can be counter-productive. By focusing on our competitors, we can end up looking for answers from them in terms of defining our unique offer. We can fall into the trap of copying them, even though our capabilities and the things that drive us are different. Or, we create a product and service that is different for the sake of it – just to stand out. We go for the gap in the market, even though we don't believe in the thing we are supposed to be offering. Or, we create an offer which we simply can't sustain. In an attempt to be different for the sake of it, we can end up making promises we can't keep. The outcome is unsustainable and incongruent with our values and the values of the people we work with. All of this effort, just to get one up on our competitors!

It's also dangerous, because all this attention on the competition takes our focus and resources away from servicing our customers. While we're busy playing 'mine's bigger than yours,' our customers are losing faith, and looking elsewhere. We lose focus on the people we're here to help and on whom we depend for our survival, and start obsessing about something we have no control over: our competitors.

Let me take you back to 1988 again. When I first started in marketing, I was working for a large multinational consumer goods company. As I mentioned in Chapter 1, I worked in an open plan office. It was my second week and one of my colleagues warned me that the Managing Director was doing the rounds and would be 'testing me' on my market share figures. Alan Modem (not his real name of course) was a Welshman, but he had lived for a time in the U.S. and had adopted a rather weird mid-Atlantic accent, which I found unsettling.

"Well hi there Justin," Alan began in his *'Radio Fab FM'* accent, "tell me, how's Brand X trending nationally this month?"

"Oh hello Alan, it's funny you should ask that, but I was just reviewing the numbers when you stopped by," I replied innocently, "The good news is that we are up by 0.2% nationally month on month, and up 0.1% year-on-year, on a moving annual total basis that is." Maths wasn't exactly my strong suit, so I thought I'd throw that last bit in for good measure.

"Gee that's just swell," Alan replied, "Do you happen to know how we are doing in Wales and the West Country?"

Oops. I didn't – I had only swotted up on London, Scotland, and East Anglia. "Oh well," I thought, "I'll just have to make it up."

"Good news there too Alan – we're up a whopping 0.3% this month," I lied through my teeth.

"Wow that's awesome – keep up the good work Justin," Alan commented, as he sauntered off to harass another marketer on her Nielsen figures.

The reality was that my company – like all its competitors, and indeed the entire FMCG world – had an unhealthy addiction to market share. We lived or died by it. It was driven by machismo, as 99% of senior managers were men.

It sapped our power to create. By focusing our attention on the opposition, that's where our power went. It leaked out of every pore in the organisation, instead of going into growing our potential to deliver amazing things for our consumers. With all the time, money, and effort we spent measuring the size of our (ahem) 'product,' we had fewer resources to actually service our consumers. We were effectively giving our power away in this climate of competition.

Sadly this obsession with market share doesn't seem to have gone away, even nearly 30 years later. We still get off on having a bigger one than our competitors.

Own Your Uniqueness

Where does this thinking come from? It originates from our unwavering belief in scarcity, which we've all been brought up on. There's not enough to go around, so steal it off someone else before it's all gone.

So here's another model to consider. There's plenty to go around, because what you have to offer is so unique, so special, so precious, that no one else can offer it. You, and you alone, possess a gift that helps people in a completely unique way. There's absolutely no one else on the planet that can think or create in the way you can, so what you offer can't be copied, borrowed or stolen. Because only you know (intuitively) how to do the thing you do. It's like having an invisible patent. No one can touch your unique gift. And this applies not only to an individual, but also to a company or brand.

When we approach our market, we can now think and act differently. There's plenty of space for other players, because what we offer can't be replicated, and the people we offer it to intuitively know that they have made the right choice because they share the same values as the individual, company, or brand they bought it from. They trust us to deliver.

We can even look at our competitors as potential partners. Richard Branson has been doing this for years because he knows his Purpose and is comfortable in his own skin. Of course, he doesn't get it right all the time, but he understands his Mission. Despite all the challenges of being dyslexic, he has come through as a massive success story. He doesn't get flustered by bigger and stronger competitors. Instead he focusses on what he's good at, and gives it to his customers. And then he looks around for other like-minded players in the market to team up with.

Rather than obsessing about who's better between us, or our competitors, we need to learn to understand, accept, and use our unique talents and gifts. That way, we can obsess about the best way to deliver this gift to our willing and grateful clients.

The Power of Self-Belief

While all this might sound a little radical coming from a man who was once described by a recruiter as a 'dyed in the wool blue-chip marketer,' it's actually just an exercise in self-belief. It doesn't matter if you're looking for the next step in your career, running a small business, or managing a brand – you have to back yourself and your own beliefs.

Asking the consumer what he or she wants is a great reason to avoid making tough decisions. I know – I've used that tool myself.

"96% of consumers said that stronger hair was a desirable feature, but only 80% said that softer hair was what they wanted. So we'll have to cancel the 'softer hair' ad campaign, because we'd be missing out on all those consumers who want stronger hair."

The fact that you've developed a breakthrough in shampoo technology to deliver 'softer hair,' and you'd be the only one in the market to offer it is ignored. The '96% of consumers' has you caught in the headlights, and you are wracked by fear.

Similarly, the process of obsessing about what the competition is up to is another way of dodging the responsibility to act.

"They're too strong in that area for us to take them on."

"Their advertising budgets are too large."

"Their relationship with Supermarket X is too strong for us to have a chance of securing a listing."

It's mesmerising to segment our customers and to gaze at our competitors with fear and awe. It's also paralysing. It stops us from recognising what we stand for, and what we are really capable of. And at the end of the day, that's the only thing that really matters – to discover our true selves.

When we do that we open up a world of possibilities. We get a glimpse of our potential, and see what we could be if we only allow ourselves to dream – if only we can ignore the distraction of market data luring us to follow the crowd, or the competitors luring us to stay away from an idea that we were born to deliver on.

This is no ego trip, this is your path to success, and every successful person knows it. It's about self-leadership and the self-confidence to be your true self. It's about recognising that to share your unique gift is not just about making money, but is also an act of *doing service* for others. Because to allow market stats or strong competitors to deter you from delivering what you were born to deliver means not only missing out on the profits, but letting your customers and clients down.

In summary the new approach to business can be summed up in one phrase:

"It's all about you – not them."

Chapter 4
The Power of Purpose

I've explained why I believe you need to shift your focus from trying to second-guess the needs of your market, and the activities of your competitors, to focusing on *you,* and what you're really here to do for your clients.

Now I'd like to go a stage further, and suggest to you that it's absolutely essential that you get clear on your Purpose before you spend another cent on marketing your career, business, or brand.

Let's go back to a comment I made in Chapter 2 — when I talked about how we are moving into a new 'conscious age' — where people are looking to connect with tribes of like-minded people. Aligned with this trend is a rise in the **power of Purpose.** People are waking up to a greater sense of Purpose, and a desire to do work that *makes a difference.* And when their work is not aligned with their Purpose, they start to feel misaligned. In fact, if they're not working towards achieving their Purpose, they are becoming disgruntled, disconnected, and discombobulated. [1]

At the same time that we are searching for more meaning in our own work, our customers and consumers are looking for greater authenticity.

* Note 1: I owe a debt of gratitude to my inspirational mentor and former boss Richard Lopacki - for gifting me this word, which is a doozy. I taught my then 5-year-old daughter to share it in kindergarten class, with highly amusing results.

It's the perfect match:

- You - as the worker, owner/manager of the business, or manager of the brand discover more meaning to your work, and you gain greater clarity about how this work can make a genuine difference to your customers' lives, which you then share though your communications.

- Your potential customers – who are completely over the hype that comes from 'image marketing' – are interested to hear this authentic and heart-felt message. Something in the message strikes a chord. It sounds, looks and feels right, and they immediately trust that this is going to be right for them.

Well, not quite. There is a chance that your potential customer simply can't relate to your heart-felt message. "What on earth are you banging on about?" your prospect says to themself, "I think they've got a screw loose."

In this case they think your *why* is pretty weird, and they can't relate to it. So they walk away.

"Oh no, we've lost a potential customer!" I hear you cry.

"Great," I reply, "because that customer was about to become the worst pain-in-the-arse you have ever known. Nothing would have been good enough for them. You would have constantly struggled to meet their needs and deliver what they value. In short, they would have been a nightmare, because they doesn't *get* you. In fact, no matter what you do for them, they never will get you, because they don't share your beliefs and values. You've just dodged a bullet by telling the truth."

Purpose is the great leveller. It seeks out like-minded souls. It reveals more about people in a few sentences than an entire operations manual. But to share your Purpose involves opening up to the truth about who you really are, in a way that business people haven't needed to do for hundreds or possibly thousands of years. It requires us to be *vulnerable* in a way that doesn't seem to fit with the term 'professional.'

What are the benefits of being 'on Purpose?'

I believe that success in the early 21st Century hinges on us being clear on and communicating our Purpose. There are so many benefits to having a clearly defined Purpose, it could probably fill an entire book. So I'll focus on my Top 8:

1. Purpose gives us the clarity to see where we are heading

When we don't know why we're doing something, we can feel lost and listless. This is as true for someone's career as it is for a business or brand. Without the clarity to see the bigger goal behind what we are aiming for (beyond money or success), we end up drifting. Purpose gives us that clarity, and with it, a clear goal to strive for.

2. Purpose motivates us to achieve more

It has been said many times before: the only person holding us back from success is our own self. But when we discover our Purpose and we turn this into a Mission that explains how we will use our Purpose to help others, something powerful happens. It's like electricity coursing through our veins – we fire up with an invisible spark. Nothing seems impossible and we surge forward. If you've found real Purpose in the work you do, you'll know what I'm talking about. If you haven't, then think back to a time when you were listening to your favourite piece of uplifting music. Or consider when you witnessed your favourite sporting team winning. You get the same endorphin rush when you are working on a Purpose, and when you know that your work has the potential to make a real difference to someone's life.

3. Purpose makes decision-making easier

When we are on Purpose we make decisions intuitively. We seem to know instantly if the answer is 'yes' or 'no.' Rather than going on a logical merry-go-round of 'yes, no, maybe,' to the point where we feel like our heads are going to explode, we can relax and make intuitive decisions, because we can now match the right decision with a gut-felt understanding of what will work best for us in the long term.

4. Purpose encourages us to take leadership – to lead ourselves, and to lead others

This benefit has been pointed out to me by a few people, most recently my good friend Steven Arnold from Iconika.com.au.

It seemed so natural I guess I missed it. Being in command of where you are going, being self-motivated, and finding it easy to make your own decisions are all by-products of being on Purpose. And of course when that happens, it's a lot easier to inspire others to follow our lead.

5. Purpose connects us with our audience behind a common goal

Martin Luther King had a dream – and when he shared it, people responded. Most of us have a dream too. A dream that one day we'll make a real difference. When we explain this dream, we inspire like-minded people to follow us, work with us, buy from us, fund us, and so on. It makes selling easier, because people 'see' the Vision we are describing, and they feel our passion to achieve it. As a result, they want to be part of this Vision.

6. Purpose engenders trust with our audience

People buy from people, and only from people they trust.

Gone are the days when a business could simply say "Trust us, we are professionals, with an expert team who know a hell of a lot about our subject, and over 20 years of experience doing what we do – with great results – so go ahead and buy from us."

They need more than that. Much more. Without realising it consciously, deep down our audience need to know who we are, and what we stand for. They need to know that piece of information way before we start telling them how brilliant we are.

7. Purpose makes recruiting easy

Do you think Elon Musk has trouble recruiting his team? Or Richard Branson? Or (back in the day) Steve Jobs? Of course not – there are people literally falling over themselves to work for these inspirational leaders, all of who are clear on, and have articulated, their business Purpose and Mission. Everyone feels the energy that Purposeful leaders have, and they want a piece of it. So why not create it for yourself?

8. Purpose defines our uniqueness

And last – but by no means least – Purpose makes us naturally unique. No need for bells, whistles, or stardust. What you see is what you get, and what you get is pure, natural, unadulterated uniqueness.

Why? Because we are no longer afraid to tell it straight – to tell the truth about who we are, why we're here, and what we are here to do for people. In a world of 'market-followers' we make for a refreshing change with our say-it-like-it-is Vision for the world we are here to create. No one's ever going to dare call you *bland* when you are on Purpose.

How about some evidence?

"That's all good in theory - but where's the evidence?" I hear you ask.

Apart from the obvious examples of **Apple** and **Google**, where are the success stories of individuals, businesses, and brands that live by an inspirational Purpose and/or Mission?

How about **Uber**?

Their stated Purpose is:

To give people transportation as reliable as running water, everywhere for everyone.

Their authentic story about *why* they created the company is published on their website:

"On a snowy Paris evening in 2008, Travis Kalanick and Garrett Camp had trouble hailing a cab. So they came up with a simple idea—tap a button, get a ride. Whether it's a ride, a sandwich, or a package, we use technology to give people what they want, when they want it."

And this connects directly with a genuine problem they solve for their clients:

They provide a crowd-sourced solution to the issue of overpriced, hard-to-find taxis, and have revolutionised the unwieldy and monopolised taxi industry.

Uber's revenue has grown from $US1.5 billion in 2015 to a projected $US26 billion in 2016.

Or how about **Elon Musk**, the founder of **Tesla**? Tesla's long-term Mission Statement is:

"To accelerate the word's transition to sustainable energy."

Tesla's mid-term goal is:

"To accelerate the advent of sustainable transport by bringing compelling, mass-market, electric cars to market as soon as possible."

And as if this wasn't inspirational enough, Elon goes on to add:

"The long term ultimate objective – the holy grail – is to help make life multi-planetary. It sounds a bit crazy but it's going to happen, and only if people build the means to do so. We're making progress toward a greater philosophical goal while building a sound business."

I don't know about you, but that statement certainly floats *my* boat.

Tesla's revenue doubled from $US2.01 billion in 2013 to $US4.05 billion in 2015, and expanded to $7.0 billion by the close of 2016.

Having a visionary Purpose and Mission certainly does inspire people to buy from you.

Then there are the **Firms of Endearment** companies, (from the 2003 book by Jagdish Sheth, David A. Wolf and Raj Sisodia) such as:

✓ **Harley Davidson**: "Fulfilling dreams of personal freedom" - with revenues rising from $US4.9 million in 2010 to $US6 billion in 2016.
✓ **Patagonia**: "Build the best product, cause no unnecessary harm, use business to inspire and implement solutions to the environmental crisis" – with their profits tripling from 2008 to 2016.

Now the cynic might say "it takes a lot more than a pretty Mission statement to make a business successful," and that is of course true. But I believe a great Mission Statement can be the spark that lights the fire. Do all of the Firms of Endearment companies have an inspiring and relevant Mission Statement? No they don't – some have boring and/or vapid and meaningless Mission Statements – but then again, the authors of the book weren't looking at that aspect as part of their selection criteria. I believe those companies that don't have an inspiring, relevant and authentic Mission which is fully supported by the whole organisation need to develop one, and quickly, because Purpose has become very important to customers, employees, business partners, shareholders, indeed all stakeholders, and this importance is set to grow.

How do you go about developing your Purpose?

Ah, the $50 billion question (allowing for inflation). As you'll see in Chapter 7, I've developed a radical way of doing this, which involves a unique approach. But as our relationship is only 4 chapters old, I won't go into that yet – I don't want to frighten the horses. For now, let's proceed using the tried and tested, traditional, and *rational* way.

5 key questions to ask yourself to uncover your Purpose

Listed on the next page you'll find 5 questions I recommend that you ask yourself to gain insights into your professional, business, and/or brand's *why* question. But before you have a go at answering them, please read the background information under the heading 'Guide to answering the questions'.

5 insightful questions to ask yourself:

1. What do you believe in, and how does it relate to the market you work in?

2. What's the biggest problem you fix for your clients that relates to what you believe in?

3. What do you a) stand for and b) stand against in your market?

4. Who are you here to help?

5. How do you make a genuine and positive impact on your clients' lives?

Guide to answering the questions

The answers to these questions will help your prospects decide if you are the right fit for them. Most importantly, they will be able to decide if they can trust you. Then – and only then – can you can go ahead and tell them what product or service you offer and how you deliver it. As Simon Sinek says, "People don't buy what you do, they buy why you do it."

By explaining *why* first, you are asking your audience if they are 'with you' or not. If they are, then you have similar beliefs and values, and you will get along just fine. If they are not, the relationship is likely to be a disaster from start to finish. Both parties will struggle, because they don't 'get' each other.

Not explaining *why* is like going up to a complete stranger and asking them to marry you. Not terribly subtle – and highly likely to illicit a 'naff off' from the stranger.

The standard approach to marketing for most businesses is to broadcast how experienced, competent, and brilliant you, your company, and your brand are. But in reality your prospect doesn't give a monkey's doodle about how amazing you and your company are. Really they don't. They *expect* you to be good, because that's the entry-level requirement for everyone. What they really want to know is whether they can trust you to fix their problem and make their lives a whole lot better.

So the big question is this: Do your current communications – your resume / website / sales brochure / marketing collateral / social media blurb / sandwich board /etc. give insights into some or all of those five questions? If they don't, well then "Houston, we have a problem."

Before you have a crack at the questions, here's an example of how I would answer them for my own business:

1. What do you believe in – and how does it relate to the market you work in?

I believe we are all born with a unique gift that allows us to see the world, think, and act in a unique way. When we apply this gift to our work, and connect it to an inspirational Purpose and Mission, we have the power to make a real difference in the world.

2. What's the big problem you fix for your clients that relates to what you believe in?

Most people, businesses, and brands don't know what makes them unique. They haven't defined their Purpose and Mission, so they don't know what they are really capable of. As a result, they struggle to attract the clients, partner, and opportunities that are rightfully theirs.

3a) What do you stand for in your market?

I stand for 'conscious' business practices – where individuals and companies understand the Purpose behind the work they do, and turn this into a Mission – to help their clients overcome a genuine problem and make a real difference to their lives.

3b) What do you stand against in your market?

I'm against the 'old way' of marketing – where businesses and brands 'invent' a client problem, then put pressure on prospects to buy a product or service they don't actually need.

4. Who are you here to help?

I am here to help business owners, brand managers, and employees who struggle to define what makes them unique, and who don't realise the true value they can offer to their clients and business partners.

5. How do you make a genuine and positive impact on your clients' lives?

I give my clients the clarity to understand their Purpose and Mission, and with it the knowledge of what makes them unique. I give them the courage to explain their uniqueness. I give them the confidence to define what they can do to make a real difference for others. I show them how to attract the right customers and business partners, and to create a broader tribe of like-minded people.

So now it's your turn.

OK – so I did do a good deal of soul-searching and had help from a number of fantastic coaches to get me to the point where I could answer these questions. You may not feel like you have all the answers yet, but give it a go. The trick is to relax and answer from your heart and/or gut (whichever feels easier). This will start you down the road to working out your work Purpose and client Mission. Later, I'll show you a technique that makes answering these questions a lot easier, and gives you deeper, and more authentic answers.

But first give this 'rational approach' a try, so you can see the difference later. For the time being let's see what answers you come up with.

1. What do you believe in – and how does it relate to the market you work in?

_____

_____

_____

2. What's the big problem you fix for your clients that relates to what you believe in?

_____

_____

_____

3a. What do you stand for in your market?

_____

_____

_____

3b. What do you stand against in your market?

_____

_____

_____

4. Who are you here to help?

_____

_____

_____

5. How do you make a genuine and positive impact on your clients' lives?

_____

_____

_____

Of course it's not enough to just discover and share your Purpose and Mission. You (and your team) have to actually *live* your Purpose through everything you say and do in your work and business. In other words, you have to walk the talk. More about that in Chapter 8.

Congratulations - you have now created an outline for how to explain what you do for your customers, partners and stakeholders – along with why you do it – in a way that can create interest, excitement, and engender trust. We'll be dialling this up later using a new technique.

For now, let's take a look at what I propose should replace 'traditional marketing.'

I call it 'Purposing', for the simple reason that it involves marketing intuitively and on Purpose.

Chapter 5
Long Live *Purposing*

Let me introduce a new word into the English Language: **Purposing** (*Pur•pos•ing*).

Definition of Purposing:

Purposing is the act of delivering your unique gift in an authentic, unique, and Purposeful way, to an audience that genuinely needs it. It is founded on you understanding and articulating your business Purpose (your 'why') and customer Mission in a way that creates a deep connection with like-minded partners, who are inspired to join your tribe, because they share your beliefs and values.

65

Purposing is the process of working 'on Purpose' to solve a genuine problem and deliver a solution that brings real benefits to the people you are here to help. Purposing connects sellers with buyers in a natural, intuitive way. It's a win-win practice that adds value to all parties concerned.

It's quite different from this **definition of Marketing** (by Philip Kotler):

Marketing is the science and art of exploring, creating, and delivering value to satisfy the needs of a target market at a profit. Marketing identifies unfulfilled needs and desires. It defines, measures, and quantifies the size of the identified market and the profit potential. It pinpoints which segments the company is capable of serving best and it designs and promotes the appropriate products and services.

What's the difference?

The big difference here is that marketing takes an 'us and them' approach, with the seller targeting the market to gain a profit. Yes, there are benefits to both parties, but the primary focus is on the seller making a profit. I mean that's the whole point of being in business right? It is also a rational process requiring the people offering the product or service to explain 'what' they offer and 'how' they deliver it in a unique way, in order to create a 'point of difference' between them and their competitors. The customer then picks the product or service that sounds most attractive. They can often be disappointed, as when they start working with or using that person, company, or brand, they may find their values don't match, which leads to buyer remorse.

In contrast, *purposing* is a more intuitive approach that connects two like-minded parties together for mutual gain. It requires the owner or manager of the business, brand, or career to understand and explain *why* they do what they do, and how this translates into a service that can solve a genuine problem their customers have. The customer then picks the product or service they believe will best solve their problem, and the one that aligns with their own personal and professional values.

Traditional marketing can be explained in simple terms with the Venn diagram model shown below. The market and/or client is represented by the black circle, and the product/service by the blue circle. The overlapping point between the two circles is where the demand/need connects with what the product or service offers. Within this space you 'create' your U.S.P. (Unique Selling Proposition), to differentiate yourself from, and in competition with, other players in the market.

Traditional Marketing

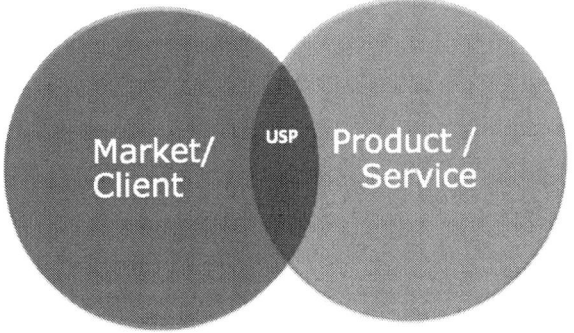

Purposing introduces a third dimension: 'you.' This is represented in the diagram below by the orange circle. This is the intuitive part of the equation, and it's where you start the process.

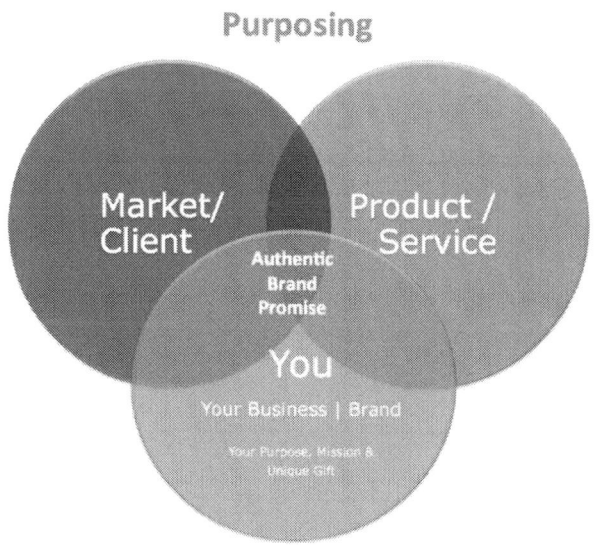

Rather than starting by looking at the market to see where the gaps are, you start by exploring your own Purpose to determine the problem you are here to solve. It's from an understanding of your Purpose – what you are really capable of, and what you are here to achieve – that you discover the problem you solve. You then look at your market very differently; not in terms of how you can target segments to your advantage, but in terms of how you solve a genuine problem that people have.

You still assess the demand for what you decide you are best equipped to offer people, and you can modify your offering to ensure it has stronger appeal. But what you are **not** doing is targeting a gap in the market just because it's there, and because no one else is filling it. That's a trap, because in reality you may not be genuinely qualified to fill that gap. You also might find that over time you (and your team) simply aren't motivated enough to do this work. Interest wanes and it starts to become a chore. Eventually you ask yourself, what happened to that dream I used to have of doing something I feel passionate about?

By contrast *purposing* is about understanding how you can solve the one problem you, your business, brand, and/or team were meant to solve, using your unique way of thinking, so that like-minded customers come flocking to you, because they intuitively know you can help them. It's about developing or adapting your product, service, or resume so that it's on Purpose, on Mission, and solves your customers' genuine problem, in a way that is uniquely yours.

At the point where these three circles overlap is where you will find your tribe. It's also where you add the most value, and where it becomes much easier to sell to your clients. That's because instead of targeting them, you are meeting them on common ground. They were looking for you, and you were looking for them. They have a problem, and you have a solution that you were born to give them. It turns the current approach on its head.

Authentic Brand Promise

Rather than a *Unique Selling Proposition* or a 'point of difference' of old - which is uniqueness founded on its difference from your competition, the new measure is your Authentic Brand Promise (ABP). This comes from your Purpose, rather than an invented point of differentiation from your competitors.

It's *authentic*, because it's born from who you are (as an individual, or a company, or as the brand's personality), and it's a *promise* you make to improve their lives in some way. An ABP is a commitment to making a genuine difference to people's lives. As far as **purposing** is concerned, this commitment to making a difference to your customers, tribe, and community is everything.

Working 'on Purpose' is about having 'skin in the game' and understanding the deeper reason *why* you're working. Having a Purpose and a Mission keeps you, your company, and/or your brand honest. It's the foundation for something real, powerful, and palpable. Purpose isn't some sort of fad that will come and go – Purpose is here to stay. And rather than it being an add-on, I believe it will soon sit at the centre of businesses, branding, and/or career planning. Everything will start and finish with Purpose.

Understanding who **you** are – whether that means 'you' as an individual, 'you' as a business, or 'you' as a brand – is the starting point for a new kind of dialogue. This authentic approach makes for a powerful connection between you and all the other stakeholders: your business partners, your team, your customers, and your shareholders. That's what Purpose brings – an authenticity and genuineness that's been lacking from traditional marketing.

Purposing is about making a deeper connection with, and a deeper commitment (or promise) to your customer. It's an authentic and genuine commitment, because your promise is based on what you believe in, what you're good at, and your higher Purpose to make a difference. Nothing is more authentic than that.

Conscious Business

The concept of *purposing* I am proposing is strongly influenced by *Conscious Capitalism* – a book published in 2013 by John Mackey and Raj Sisodia. It followed in much the same vein as *Firms of Endearment*, first published in 2003 by Jagdish Sheth, David A. Wolf and Raj Sisodia. Both books talk about the power of Purpose to move business people away from a pure focus on revenue and profits, towards working for a higher ideal that inspires people to work together for a common cause and shared ideals.

It's Your Responsibility

Purposing is about accepting the responsibility that you were born with a Purpose and that your Purpose is to make a difference. When you get clear on that, the game changes. When you stop focussing on everyone else (the market and your competitors), and stop worrying about fitting in – that's when the real fun begins. When you can say "I'm here for a reason, I only have a short amount of time to deliver on it," you really start to make a difference.

That's why *starting with you* is so important. To be successful in today's market, you need to first be clear on who you are and why you are here *before* you help others. It's like the safety demonstration that's always delivered before an aircraft takes off. You are instructed to **put the oxygen mask on yourself, before helping others.** Why? Because if you're dead, you can't help the people who need you, and rely on you for help.

The 'Why Foundation'

Once you've worked out your Purpose, or your *why*, it becomes the foundation for any new product, service, or brand you launch, and/or any career change you make. It's like the concrete foundation of a house upon which you place the pillars.

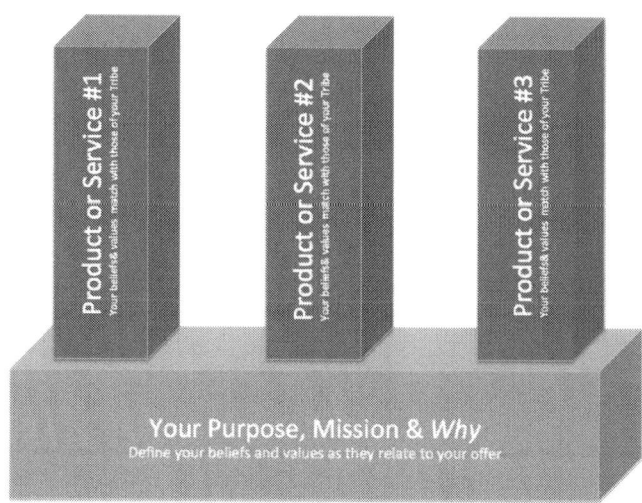

Your job is to define your beliefs and values in terms of the work that you do and/or the product or service you offer. Then when it comes to launching a new product or service, or moving into a new career or line of work, you only go with the ones that align with your beliefs and values. And your tribe (formerly your 'target market') then gets to decide if its own beliefs and values line up with yours. If they do, then it makes the decision to buy from you and/or work with you that much easier.

Each pillar represents what you offer, and how you offer it, in a way that supports and promotes your *why*. If it doesn't fit in the groove created by your *why*, it topples over. If it stands firm, it's a good fit.

In other words, the decision on what you offer is based on *why*, not *what.* It's a much easier way of working – it causes a lot less internal conflict and stress, and ensures you can turn up to work as you, not someone you've manufactured for the role.

In practice, this means checking with yourself (and/or your team) to see if your new idea or direction fits with your beliefs and drivers. Are you doing it for purely monetary reasons, or are you genuinely committed to it? Does it fit with your Purpose and/or the culture of the company? Does the culture of the company you are considering joining fit your own beliefs? If the answer is no, you could find yourself struggling a few months after launch, or after taking up your new position, because it just doesn't fit with what drives you, who you are, and what you believe in. So before considering launching a new product, service, brand and/or career, I recommend you check that it passes the 'Why Foundation' Test.

The Four Key Steps to *Purposing*

Working out who you are and what you're capable of is the first step to developing a career, business, or brand that can make a real difference in the world. It's also the gateway to discovering greater happiness, satisfaction, and success in your work.

Once you have a strong belief in yourself/your company/your brand in terms of what you are capable of, you then have an insight into what you offer that's truly unique. Rather than trying to 'fill a gap in the market,' you now have a genuine Vision on how you can make a difference. This is the fundamental step needed, before you can work out how the other pieces of the jigsaw fit together.

The second step is to work out the **Purpose** behind your work. This is the deeper reason – the thing that drives you or your business to work harder to achieve your goal. I'm not talking about revenue or profits, but the deeper *why* that drives you. It might be to change the way things are currently done in your market, or to make an improvement for your clients. The best Purpose statements are inspirational, altruistic, and outcome-focused. They explain why you, your business, and/or your brand exist. For instance, Elon Musk's business Purpose might be to "become the catalyst that eliminates fossil fuel usage." **Purpose explains *why* you do the work you do,** and has the potential to drive you and/or your team.

The third step is to define your ***Mission***, which explains what you plan to do with your Purpose, and the outcome you want to deliver to your audience. In other words, your Mission outlines what you will do for your clients, your partners, and your tribe. It answers the question "what will you do to make a difference?" It doesn't matter whether you are running a not-for-profit charity, or you're selling an energy bar – both have the potential to change the game. In the case of Elon Musk, his initial Mission was to "accelerate the word's transition to sustainable energy." This has now been updated to a 'Holy Grail' Mission to "help make life multi-planetary." **Mission explains what you are here to do for people.**

The final step is to define exactly who your **ideal client** is. This is easy, because you already know your Mission – so it's a short step from knowing what you are here to do for people, to defining exactly who it is that needs your help the most. It's about developing a thumbnail sketch of the person you are here to help and defining the genuine problem they have, that you are uniquely qualified to solve for them. Not the invented problem that is made up to create demand for a product, but the problem you, your business and/or your brand was born to solve. Once you've done that, you can develop or adapt your product or service to make it work even better to meet that need, while all the time working on your Purpose.

So to recap, here are the four key steps involved in developing your Authentic Brand Promise (ABP) using *purposing* as your guide:

Step 1: Unearth the Real You

Work out what you stand for (or if a company or brand, what your beliefs/values are), what you're capable of, and what your 'secret ingredient' and uniqueness is.

Step 2: Define Your Purpose

Armed with a better understanding of who you are (as an individual, organisation and/or brand), you can now explore and define the higher Purpose behind the work you do.

Step 3: Define your Mission

Then translate your internal Purpose into an external Mission, that explains what you'll do to change the way things are currently done. This is so you can improve the lives of your clients, business partners (your team, suppliers, collaborators), communities, and tribe.

Step 4: Define your Ideal Client

Now you know what you are here to improve or invent – you can define the problem you are here to fix, and who your ideal client is. This is a far cry from targeting someone to extract profit. Instead you are now identifying the person who needs your help the most; to solve a problem that you are uniquely qualified to solve.

The emergence of 'Total Intelligence' (TI)

I said earlier that I believe traditional marketing to be a predominately rational process. In contrast, *purposing* requires the use of emotional, intuitive, **and** rational thinking. And by using all three ways of thinking we are actually connecting to a higher level of intelligence.

Let me explain. For around a hundred years, the world used an IQ (intelligence quotient) to decide how smart people were. An IQ measures someone's reasoning and problem-solving capacity against the average for their age. In other words, it only measures logical capacity.

In 1964 Michael Beldoch proposed another measurement, EQ (emotional quotient) or EI (emotional intelligence). This is defined by Wikipedia as:

"The capability to recognise one's own, and other people's emotions,

- To discriminate between different feelings and label them appropriately,

- To use emotional information to guide thinking and behaviour,

- To manage and/or adjust emotions to adapt environments or achieve one's goals."

To function effectively with other human beings, you clearly need EQ. Yet for a long time we have undervalued EQ, and have continued to place people with a low EQ in positions of power.

While there are many examples I could use here, Donald Trump seems like a good example at time of writing (May 2017). As Wikipedia points out, "studies have shown that people with high EI have greater mental   health, job   performance, and leadership skills."

A third measure of intelligence is now emerging: 'intuitive intelligence' or II, for want of a better acronym.   Also   known   as   'subconscious intelligence,' II has been written about for the past 10 years or so, and refers to the ability of the brain to make analogies, comparisons, and associations subconsciously, to process a large quantity of data in record time and rapidly analyse a situation. (Reference: histoiredintuition.com).

According to thehumancompany.com it is defined as the combination of 4 abilities:

1. The ability to think holistically

2. The ability to think paradoxically – the paradox being that empowering people and relationships are the key to better financial results, rather than better economic management *per se*

3. The ability to listen and connect to oneself and others

4. The ability to lead by influence rather than design

So when engaged in *purposing*, we need to combine all three forms of intelligence together into one neat package, like this:

IQ + EI + II = TI (Total Intelligence)

TI can be defined as the ability to trust (and listen to) your emotional and intuitive intelligence – then to use your rational IQ to work out how to use this information to solve what previously appeared to be an impossible problem. It's the act of leveraging intuition, emotion, and rationale to springboard beyond 'normal' thinking, to take it to a higher place.

TI could well be the higher level of thinking needed to get us humans out of the current environmental, economic, social, and political 'pickle' we appear to have got ourselves into.

On a slightly less lofty note, it can certainly help **you** get yourself out of your own particular business pickle – if you want it to.

But it only works if you're prepared to 'imagine your future,' and create a Vision for what you will achieve. Without a Vision, you are destined to drift. When you have a Vision and you put it into action, great things happen. Or as Joel A. Barker says, "Vision with action can change the world." We'll be doing an exercise to create a Vision for your business, brand, or career in Chapter 9.

Building your Brand using TI.

Business over the past few hundred years has been driven almost exclusively by rational or 'head thinking.' But as EI and II become more important, this brings the idea of 'heart thinking' into play for people in business. This way of thinking was until quite recently reserved for the creative arts – it had no play in core business. But players like Apple and Google have changed things. The next step involves combining head and heart thinking, to create a new, holistic, and conscious business offer. It's a 'whole brain' approach; it's authentic, and it explains your Mission in terms of how you help people. It blends rational planning and fluid thinking to create a flexible approach to business.

As you'll see from the chart above **traditional marketing** sits on the left of the chart, and is about using your head to think things through. It's predominately a left brain/rational process that answers the 'what' and 'how' questions, such as 'what do I offer?' and 'how do I offer it?' It's about developing a planned path, showing how to get from A to B. It's about thinking through the problem. It involves creating an image for yourself, your business, or your brand, and being clear on your objective to plot future success in a linear fashion. It's solid and dependable. But it's also unimaginative and not very creative, as it relies almost exclusively on rational thinking.

On the right is the **creative arts approach.** This is all about right brain, emotional creativity. It's about asking why, without necessarily needing to know the answer. It's fluid, emotional, and Purposeful. Feeling drives it, not rational thought. It is perfect for generating creative and entertaining performances and executions. It's not always so good at delivering solid outcomes on time, because it's fluid, and "let's face it man, you can't box me in with your outcomes and timelines, I'm a free thinker."

Purposing is a blend of the two approaches. It uses both the right and left brain to activate intuitive, emotional, *and* rational thinking, in a whole brain process. It defines the Purpose of the work and attaches this to a Mission so there is an active and effective outcome to the Purpose. It asks why, what, and how – then adds the question 'what if?' to spark the imagination. It questions 'what else is out there?' 'how else could this be done?' and 'what if we imagined something completely new?'

It's flexible, so you can change course as you move towards your objective, based on new information and new ideas you receive along the way. It's based on being authentic and true to who you really are, and taps into an intuitive knowing and reading of situations. It's the best of both worlds and delivers a smarter way of being and working.

How can you use this approach to help develop your own business, brand, or career?

Are you over-rationalising what you do for people to the point that your communications come across as dull and uninspiring? Are you being so emotive and 'touchy-feely' that you are not articulating the end-benefits of what you offer to your customer or manager?

Look at how you communicate your offer — whether that's through your website, social media, brand communications, CV and so on — and ask yourself:

"How can I explain what I offer in a more holistic way?"

"How can I bring a TI approach, so I am thinking, acting, and communicating with my head, heart, and gut?"

And are you asking yourself the most potent question of all - 'What if?'

It's important to do this because it fires the imagination, and opens you up to what could be - rather than accepting what **is.**

My Journey from Marketing to *Purposing.*

Understanding my own Purpose was the driving force for me deciding to give up a 25-year career as a marketer in 2012. I hit a brick wall; I simply couldn't carry on doing things the 'old way' any more. I could no longer bear to work in an area that I now saw as flawed, founded on spin and image. I needed to be authentic in my work, and that meant doing something very different. I had studied meditation and energy healing (including Reiki) since 2006 as a hobby, but I didn't dare to connect it with my business. What if people thought I'd gone crazy? Would they laugh at me?

So in late 2012 I created an online course that combined brand development with meditation, called *Your Authentic Business:*

justinjgcooper.com/your-authentic-business-details

It's designed to help small business owners articulate their brand story in a heart-felt, authentic, and intuitive way. I scripted the 8 videos and worksheets, then found a great company to film, direct, and post-produce it. I even found a co-presenter to help me deliver the content. And then I put it up online and expected it to sell.

Bad move – especially from an experienced marketer who knows full well that products don't just sell themselves. Sure, I put some money behind a Google ad campaign in 2013, but it was half-hearted. I managed to hand-sell the course to a few people, who got good results, but this wasn't exactly the ground-breaking, global phenomenon I had been hoping for.

I went back to marketing to bring some dollars in. It killed my spirit, and I got pretty depressed. I felt completely stuck. I couldn't move forward, and I couldn't move back. Then came the tipping point on 20th December 2013. It was a meeting with the General Manager of a boutique hotel in Sydney. I had met with his off-sider a few times and now it was the crunch meeting to get final approval to proceed. Prior to the meeting I said to myself: "I'm going to tell this guy that my methodology involves meditation. If he laughs, I'll walk away."

I felt a sense of calm going into the meeting. Normally I'd be nervous, but not this time. We chatted as I set up my laptop. He came across as slightly aloof and a little sceptical, but I ploughed on regardless. "Here goes," I thought to myself as I explained to him that the breakthrough I had discovered was to use meditation to access the subconscious mind.

He laughed. I started closing my laptop, preparing to leave.

And then he said, "The reason I'm laughing is that meditation saved my life. I had a heart attack a few years ago, and after the operation, my surgeon recommended meditation as the best way to recover and to protect myself from stress. I've been meditating regularly for years now."

I could have kissed him. And I can assure you, he wasn't my type.

There it was – my first 'live' and fee-paying client to experience my new technique. The universe had come to the party after all.

This gave me the confidence to turn my online video workshop into a live experience, and for the next two years I ran these as public 'playshops' under the name 'Unleash Your Beast.'

I had managed to escape the hamster wheel. And that's exactly what I want to help you to do now, by reading this book and doing the exercises I have provided links to.

But first you're going to need to take off the mask.

Chapter 6
Take off the Mask

Why are the ideas I'm proposing so *out there*? Why is it such a big leap to talk about Purpose, authenticity, and belief within the context of work and business?

From a young age we are taught to be 'professional' in business. And to most people this means being logical, serious, competitive (hard-nosed), and profit-focused. There's simply no room for *humanity* in the business equation. It's hard-wired into our system, thanks to generations of

Industrial-Revolution thinking, as Seth Godin points out in his book *Linchpin*. [*2]

We don't want to start caring deeply about what we do, and getting all soft and emotional, now do we? That's not what business is about! Where on earth would that lead us?

Or as C.J. from *The Fall and Rise of Reginald Perrin* would say:

"I didn't get where I am today by caring about people."

The reason it's so hard for business people to relax, be authentic, and to use their intuition to guide them, is that business hasn't been done like this for hundreds of years. The 'normal' approach to business is to rely almost exclusively on rational thinking.

Note 2: Seth Godin's excellent book Linchpin explains more on this topic of the post-industrial revolution hangover that most of us are still suffering from.

As Seth Godin points out, before the Industrial Revolution we were artisans. After it, we became cogs in the wheels of industry. But that revolution finished many years ago, and now we need to be creative, inventive, and unique in the way we approach business problems and opportunities. And that's challenging, because it's not the 'done thing' for most business people.

Of course, not all businesses take a purely rational approach – look at Google's use of meditation and sleep pods, climbing walls, and music rooms. And of course advertising and creative agencies have used creative work spaces for many years to help generate imaginative thinking. But it's certainly not mainstream yet.

So the notion of having a Purpose, being authentic, and talking about what you believe in are alien concepts to most business and branding people. But the more we ignore these potent tools, the harder it becomes to connect with and attract like-minded customers, employees, and business partners.

The problem is that we've been waging this dog-eat-dog campaign against our competitors for so long now, we don't trust any other way. And we've been so focused on the pursuit of profit as a means to an end, that we've lost sight of the bigger reason of why we started our business or career in the first place: to achieve something worthwhile.

My friend Muneesh Wadhwa runs *Humanity in Business* – and is part of a network of companies that have been inspired by the *Conscious Capitalism* movement, which I mentioned in the previous chapter. Muneesh is on a crusade to encourage larger businesses to define and live their true Purpose, and then to develop a genuine culture founded on this Purpose. His Mission is to prove to companies that a genuine corporate culture that looks after its people, is aware of its impact locally and environmentally, and actually cares about its customers, is not only good for business, but is good for profitability.

And as Simon Sinek points out, a company culture that starts by looking after its employees automatically delivers better outcomes for its customers, and generates better and more sustainable profits. His mantra is to make shareholders the last priority, rather than the first, because by putting employees first, you deliver a better experience for your customers, and so ultimately guarantee a better return for shareholders. *3

But the underlying reason we are struggling to change the way we do business is because **we are afraid to take off the mask**. This is the mask we create for ourselves as we grow up, to ensure we are not exposed as *different* or *weird*. As social beings, humans like to blend in to be accepted by others. The trouble is, when we *do* decide to stand out as an individual; we no longer know how to do it. The mask is hard to take off.

This is particularly true for those of us who have worked in larger companies, as we learn to 'play the game.' In toxic cultures we use the mask to hide our true identity. After a while we forget we are wearing it, and lose touch with who we really are.

I experienced this myself, and it's not much fun.

Note 3* You can watch Simon in full flow on this topic here: https://www.youtube.com/watch?v=3SVqbM9Nw7Q

I felt conflicted working in an organisation where the dog-eat-dog values that persisted within the organisation didn't sit well with my own belief in an open, supportive, and positive work place.

If this strikes a chord with you, and you are keen to remove the mask and embrace your Purpose, it comes with a warning. It takes courage and commitment, and when you do, the emotion involved in remembering who you really are may take you by surprise. But it's absolutely worth it.

How to remove the mask

The first step is to remember who you are. You can do this exercise as an individual, a company, or a brand team. The key is to relax and not worry about getting the 'right' outcome. As soon as you start to worry about *getting it right,* you engage with your rational brain, and close down your limbic and reptilian centres, where the answer to your true identity lies.

The truth about who you really are is hidden from your rational mind. The rational brain simply cannot process the question. It's only designed to answer two questions: 'what?' and 'how?' The rational brain has no problem processing questions like 'what is my goal this week?' and 'How am I going to achieve it?' But try asking 'why am I here?' and 'what do I stand for?' and the rational mind has a panic attack. 'I don't know' is the first answer most people come up with. And when you push people a little to provide you with an answer – as I have done many times with my own clients in the past – you tend to get predictable and generic answers.

"What does your company believe in?" I would ask.

"Honesty and integrity," would be the answer.

No sh-t Sherlock - and there was me thinking you were just in it for the money! If I had a dollar for every time a client told me their values were 'honesty and integrity' I'd have a nice line of credit at my local pub.

After reading a few books on the subject, I came to the conclusion that the person answering the question *why* does one of three things:

1. They give an answer that they subconsciously believe their parents, teachers, or any other key person of influence would approve of

2. They give an answer that their boss or team leader would approve of

3. They give an answer that they subconsciously believe the person asking the question is looking for

Or they go for a blend of 1, 2, and 3 – with rather confusing and sometimes amusing results.

They don't mean to lie or embellish the truth, they just don't have the capacity to answer such deep questions when they are in a rational state. What they don't realise is that in trying to do so, they are actually following a hidden script. It's just not realistic to ask people to explain *why* they are doing something, because the answer is hidden deep within the subconscious mind.

It is really hard to ask someone what they believe in, what they stand for, and why they are here when they are in a rational state. The answers you get will always be limited in their integrity and usefulness, no matter how many times you re-phrase the questions.

To the rational brain anything that can't be proven beyond reasonable doubt simply isn't worth the section of brain matter it's imprinted on. So any beliefs and values that do float up into the rational mind during this kind of questioning tend to be shot down in flames and discounted as 'irrational thought.' In its place, a set of generic answers tend to pop up. "There you go," the rational mind seems to say, "here are your pesky 'beliefs and values' – now can we go and do something useful now?"

But fear not - in the next chapter I'll share a new technique I've developed that gets round the problem of the rational brain being such a slave to logic and conditioning.

What prompted me to take my own mask off?

I remember it very clearly. It was mid-late 2006 when I first met Kim Fraser from The Harmony Centre. It was a weird meeting to say the least. My friend Luke warned me it would be 'different' when he invited me in to help on a project to sell a piece of land in Queensland. My role was to interview the owner of the property and to write a brand story to market the site. So far so good.

I turned up and the client was wearing a hat with hand-drawn butterflies stitched on to it.

"Oh dear," my rational mind thought.

Then I was introduced to Kim Fraser who explained that she was going to bless the meeting with a meditation before we started.

"Ah, that's not good," I thought.

She asked us all (around 8 in total) to close our eyes and relax. I did the former, but struggled with the latter. My mind went into overdrive.

"This must be a wind-up; Luke's roped me into an episode of *Candid Camera*. Who's the weird bloke in the hat? Who starts a business meeting with a séance? How can I make an excuse and leave?"

"Justin – do you have a lot of head chatter at the moment?" asks Kim.

"Sh-t, she can read minds." I think. "She can tell I think she's a weirdo. Oh sh-t, if she can read minds – she just heard me swearing."

"Um – yes, a little," I lied.

"OK – well meditating is all about the breath work. Take a slow, deep breath into your belly – then breathe out slowly," she explained.

I did this for a few breaths and my mind started to clear. I even forgot about how weird the whole thing was for a moment. And for the first time in my life I started to meditate. Sure, it was punctuated by a lot of interruptions from my rational mind. Thoughts like "what on earth are you doing?" and "get me out of here" popped up on a fairly regular basis. But I definitely started to relax, greatly helped by the slow, deep, rhythmic breathing.

The mediation ended and it was time for the client to speak. I was still having a problem with the hand-drawn butterflies stitched to his hat, but I was now in a much more relaxed state of mind, so I was happy to let it pass. He explained that he was channelling Michael's songs, and that as each new song was written he drew a butterfly and stitched it on to his hat. I started to wobble again.

"Breathe and ignore what he's saying," a soothing voice seemed to say.

He kept mentioning Michael.

"Michael is against me selling this property but I know in my heart this is the right thing to do," said the client.

"Who is this guy Michael?" I thought.

And then a strange thought hit me. "He's talking about Michael Hutchins – the lead singer of INXS!"

"What a starnge thought," my rational mind observed.

He finished his monologue and I pulled myself together. It was time to get to work. I asked him a series of questions about the property, so I had all the information I needed to create the brand story. At the end of the meeting I said my goodbyes and left with Luke.

"OK, that was really, really weird," I said to him as we headed back to our cars.

"I have so many questions right now. But there's one I need to get off my chest. Who is this Michael guy he kept referring to?"

"Oh, he was talking about Michael Hutchins from INXS. The client used to work with the band, and he now believes he is channelling the dead singer's music. He draws and stitches a butterfly to his hat each time he finishes a song."

"Woah – what?!" I gasped.

And that was the moment my mask started to slip.

Everything I'd been told about not believing anything you couldn't prove rationally disappeared in a puff of smoke. In the following weeks I met up with Kim Fraser and that started me down a path of studying meditation and energy healing.

The questions I have for you right now are these:

What prompted or will prompt you to let go of your mask?

Will it be reading this book?

Or trying your first visualisation?

Chapter 7
Discovering Your
Secret Recipe

If you've come this far with me, then you are probably curious enough to try something new. So here's my theory about the *secret recipe*.

I believe we all have our own set of innate strengths, talents and abilities – key elements that define us and make us unique. It's like a secret recipe, which, if discovered and defined, can give us access to a new level of happiness, inspiration, productivity and success.

But sadly this secret recipe is hidden from us.

It's hidden for a number of reasons. Firstly, many of us are taught not to boast about our abilities. In Australia it's called 'Tall Poppy Syndrome' and in England it's called 'Being English.' Wherever you live, I'm sure you can relate to the idea. It's the conditioning that tells us we're not good enough, and prevents us from seeing our unique strengths. To compound the problem, most schooling systems are designed to round out our weaknesses, rather than celebrate our strengths.

Of course there are exceptions to this rule, but for most of us, by the time we are given the freedom to focus on our strengths, it's too late. We've already been conditioned not to believe that we are naturally unique.

The technique I have developed gives people access to their subconscious mind quickly and easily, so they can see what their rational mind won't allow them to see. My *business visualisations* are founded on the ancient practice of meditation, and not-so-ancient practice of NLP (Neuro Linguistic Programming). What makes the process 'new' is that it combines subconscious intuition with rational business thinking. The visualisations are delivered either via audio recordings or at face-to-face sessions.

Don't panic – I'm not asking you to join in a séance or to perform a human sacrifice. It's just a meditation. It's not nearly as 'woo-woo' as people thought it was in the past. Science is now catching up with the enormous benefits meditation brings. Many high-profile business leaders regularly use meditation and mindfulness to relieve stress and increase creative thinking.

My downloadable version involves an 11-minute exercise in which participants listen to a commentary that asks them to imagine themselves going on a journey, set to relaxing background music. As soon as the track finishes, they are invited to answer a short questionnaire in plain English asking them to explain what they visualised and/or imagined during the exercise. This is used to help them articulate their true personality and innate strengths, the Purpose behind their work, their Mission, and to describe the ideal customer for the work they do. Because they are relaxed and in a mediative state, this gives them the ability to delve into their subconscious, ensuring the answers they give come from a deeper place, and are genuine and authentic. The whole exercise only takes around 30-45 minutes to complete.

I have guided over 250 people through this process over the past four years, and I am still amazed by how effective it is at opening people up to deeper and more intuitive answers. Participants are often surprised by how accurate their subconscious responses are. Their answers feel intuitively right, yet have eluded them in the past. After years of struggling to explain themselves they can finally articulate their hidden strengths and the Purpose behind the work they do. The answers they provide after a *visualisation* go so much deeper than they had expected. It's often an emotional experience to finally remove the mask.

The most important thing to note is that **anyone** can do a *visualisation*. I've had people come to one of my events who have been very sceptical, but who have received powerful insights and clarity. The key requirement is to have an open mind, and to be willing to give it a try -— because it doesn't work if you allow your conscious mind to sabotage the process.

So here's your chance to try this technique out for yourself.

Just go to: justinjgcooper.com/animal-totem-visualisation and follow the prompts to access your free *Animal Totem Visualisation*. This is a fun exercise designed to uncover your hidden strengths and capabilities through the metaphor of an animal. It's the most effective way I've found to help remove the mask.

Now before you try this, there's a good chance you're already thinking about an animal. That's because the conscious mind wants to take control of things and *get a result*. In the hundred or so times I have run this exercise, there have only ever been a few cases where someone got the animal they were thinking of. I've had elephants, bears, wolves, badgers, pigs, and even a stingray. So please, let go of the thought that you can control what you find, and let the animal find you!

These visualisations are about getting you to let go and allow the truth to come through about who you really are. Because once you know what your animal totem is, you have an insight into the character traits that this animal brings, and uncover some important information about yourself that you didn't realise.

It can also work at a business or brand level. You can use this technique to define the culture of your business or the personality of your brand.

So why not give it a go? Click on the prompts and see what happens. You might be surprised by the animal you get. But I guarantee you that when you sit with the knowledge of what your animal totem is for a few days or weeks, you'll intuitively know that it's right for you, your business, and/or your brand.

Once you've done that, come back and start reading again, because I want to tell you more about your secret ingredient.

Once you've completed your answers, you have the option to request a fact sheet that explains what your animal totem means. You can also request further help and advice to understand how to use the information you uncover about your animal totem to develop your career, business, or brand.

The interesting thing about animal totems is that they provide a living metaphor for us to relate to. Unlike some of the other brand and client profiling tools used by marketers and creative agencies, such as avatars and cars, animals tend to have more personality, so you can have fun and play with the idea. It also makes for a more intuitive experience, as humans tend to have an invisible bond with certain animals.

What to do when you discover your totem?

I was working with a client recently to help him define the Purpose behind his start up business, and I suggested we run through the animal totem exercise. He hesitated, saying: "Well I already meditate regularly, and have done a similar exercise, and I already know that my animal totem is an eagle."

A little voice inside my head said, "No it's not." So I suggested we do the exercise anyway to see what showed up. I explained that animal totems can change throughout our lives, depending on what we need at that particular point in our journey. He agreed and we ran the session. Sure enough when he had completed the exercise he didn't 'meet' an eagle – he met a large brown bear.

The realisation for him was transformational. He had been using an overseeing, strategic and creative approach to his start-up, in the style of the eagle animal totem. He had run into problems, and he didn't feel connected with the operational aspect of the launch. He realised that he needed to be more involved, more grounded in the activities, and take more of a leadership role. All these traits are consistent with the bear animal totem, but not with the eagle. This gave him new impetus to look at the launch with fresh eyes and to take greater ownership of the key elements involved.

That's why I found the idea of using animal totems so appealing. They have been used for millennia by different societies as a form of healing, and as a way of explaining our innate strengths using a metaphor.

It's a simple metaphor to remind us of who we really are. It highlights key strengths and capabilities that we have either forgotten about or have overlooked. The fact sheet you can access describes the strengths and characteristics of your totem, along with tips on how you can use your totem to work more instinctively.

The trick is to let the information sink in over a few days or a week so you can discern what is most relevant to your current situation. Then you can look at everything you are currently doing and communicating in your career, business, or with your brand; and decide what aspects are aligned, and misaligned with who you truly are. **It is the first building block to creating a career, business, or brand that is founded on who you really are – not on what you think people want you to be**. It's an opportunity to reveal your true self and give your audience something genuine, heartfelt, and naturally unique.

If you'd like me to send you a fact sheet that explains what your animal totem means, please use this link: justinjgcooper.com/at-fact-sheet

If you'd like more help understanding what your animal totem means and how you can use the information to apply this to your working life, you can also book a coaching session with me by using this link: justinjgcooper.com/coaching-sessions

All of this is designed to give you more information about the unique way that you do things as an individual, business, or brand. Finding this 'secret ingredient' is really important, because it gives you important clues to how to market yourself in a way that will ensure you stand out from the crowd. It's about letting go of your preconceptions about who you are supposed to be, and allowing the truth of who you really are to come through. It's like peeling an onion – you have to peel back a few layers before you find the golden nugget of truth. OK, so I appreciate most onions don't actually have gold nuggets at their centre, but please go with me on this one!

It's actually a really simple process – "it's not rocket science," as an old boss of mine used to say.

The act of taking off the mask can be quite sudden, or it can take time. It really depends on the individual and what they have been through in their life. It can be tough, there can be tears; or it can be as simple as waking from a dream.

What you do next is up to you. You have a decision – to go back to your old way of doing things, or to push through and discover what's on the other side.

Some decide on the former, and they go back to what they perceive as the 'safety' of their old way of being. The trouble is that once the mask has been removed, no matter how many times it is put back on, it never seems to sit as comfortably as it did when it was first glued into place. Eventually it becomes too hard to keep up the façade, and cracks begin to appear in the mask. That's when you can't help but take it off, and that normally corresponds with a crisis of some sort.

So my advice for you if you don't feel quite ready is to take 'baby steps' to move from the old to the new you. That doesn't guarantee you not having a 'crisis' (I've had a few of those myself in the past), but it will help you pick up the pieces faster after the event and get going down a new path.

Who else has tried these visualisations?

To date I have used this visualisation technique to help three types of people:

1. **People struggling in their career** who feel uninspired and low in confidence.

2. **Business owners looking for direction** and inspiration, and who want to get clear on what makes their offer genuinely unique, so they can attract like-minded customers, employees and business partners.

3. **Entrepreneurs planning a start-up**, who want a more unique and sustainable brand positioning.

While I have to date only used this technique with individuals, I see the potential for it to be used within companies to define culture and to develop more authentic brands. I have already experimented with a colleague of mine, and he was able to project the personality of a brand he was working on. It has allowed him to develop the brand from a deeper place of intuition and knowing. I see brand teams using this mindfulness technique to create more engaging, authentic, intuitive, and unique brands. Wouldn't it be refreshing to build a consumer brand from the heart, rather than based purely on image?

I also see a great opportunity to help team leaders looking to inspire their team by discovering their own unique style, and I plan to work with larger organisations to help them develop better internal cultures and communications. I believe this technique will one day be used widely to develop greater motivation, teamwork, and creativity.

When I have conducted these visualisations in a group, there has been a 'halo effect' that comes into play, which creates a group awareness, consensus, and a shared bond. This has broader implications for how groups can collectively collaborate to understand that we are actually on the same page.

What are the benefits?

Clarity and motivation are the two most common answers I get when I ask people what they get from doing these business visualisations. They find it extremely liberating to discover that they are saying or writing a deeper truth from within. It seems to just come out unexpectedly. Often there are feelings and beliefs that have remained hidden for many years. I remember one person asking me, 'how did you get me to say that?' as if I were some sort of magician. I explained that the answers were already inside his head; I merely facilitated the process of him being able to express them.

When people act on the information they receive, it's like a weight has been lifted from them. They become freer, more relaxed, and happier. When we are relaxed, we perform better. Ask any athlete or musician: when you are tense you can't perform at your true peak, but when you are relaxed you can. They become more inspired about what they are doing, and this in turn makes it easier for them

119

to inspire those around them. There's no doubt that great leaders inspire others by first being inspired by the idea themselves.

Ultimately being 'on Purpose' means becoming more productive. When you share your Purpose and your Mission you inspire people to work with you, and to work harder. Your own productivity, and the productivity of the people around you, goes through the roof.

So Purpose isn't some kind of nebulous, nice to have, stick-in-the-bottom-of-the-drawer kind of thing. It's here to stay, and it's going to become more important in the future, because Purpose ultimately means profit. That's why I believe Purpose is the 'new black.'

By now you should have an insight into what you, your company and/or your brand stand for, along with an understanding of your innate skills, abilities, and personality.

It's time to connect who you are to your Purpose.

Chapter 8
Unearth Your Purpose

I believe the work we do has a greater Purpose behind it, which runs deeper than simply 'earning a crust.' Most of us are aware of something driving us when we are younger, but over time we become disheartened, and convince ourselves it's just not worth the hassle to chase the dream we once had.

Or in the case of a business or a brand, the ideals on which they were founded become corrupted, in an attempt to drive more profitability. The outcome is a person, business, or brand that has lost his, her, or its heart.

However it seems more and more people are now waking up to their Purpose. It's like an itch that just won't go away until they scratch it.

One of the biggest benefits of being 'on Purpose' in a work sense (i.e. having clarity of Purpose for the work you do) is that it reminds us that the real reason for working is not to succeed for the sake of it, but to succeed for the people we are here to help. It makes us realise that this gift we have isn't just for our own gratification, but for the people it is designed to serve. It gives us a natural, altruistic drive to try harder for our customers and business partners.

The imperative of making a difference comes with the territory of Purpose, because you have a duty to use your innate abilities and hidden gifts to help others. Of course, there are plenty of personal benefits to being 'on Purpose'. As we discussed earlier, it settles you and gives you clarity, which removes the feelings of overwhelm, confusion, and lack of direction that can descend on us at times when we're trying to decide what direction to go in. It also brings the potential for greater success by making us more motivated, inspirational, and proactive. That's the biggest benefit of being 'on Purpose'.

How does all this talk of Purpose relate to the issue of *Marketing Being Dead?*

As I said earlier, the term 'marketing' presupposes that the most important person in the equation is your customer, but I don't believe this – the most important person is *you* (or your business and/or brand). I say this because if you base your business success on finding out what customers want, you will be trusting your success to 'rear-view mirror thinking.' That's because customers can only tell you what they want based on what has been available in the past. *They* don't know that you've just invented a brand new out-of-the-box, change-the-game, shake-up-the-market product or service. They don't know what you know. They don't have your secret recipe. But if they believe in your Purpose, and they like the way you have packaged up your resume, business, product, or service, and you have priced it right, they certainly **will** buy it!

I talked earlier about the importance of putting the oxygen mask on yourself, before attempting to help others, and that's why it's so important to understand your Purpose and your Mission before you start helping, marketing to, and/or selling to your customer.

The Power of Truth

Once you accept that happiness and success is not about giving the market what it thinks it wants, but about giving it what you were born to deliver, a funny thing happens. You stop trying to conform, and you become free to deliver something that is uniquely yours.

And now it gets really interesting. By discovering your true self (or your authentic business or brand promise), it's like being reunited with your long lost twin – you step into the most accurate and efficient form of you there is. Patterns of old behaviour created by conditioning fall away. Over time your rational mind accepts the subconscious information you are receiving, and it learns to trust it more and more. It's a process of unfolding the truth.

As you step into the truth of who you really are, you discover a new comfort zone. This is where you do your best work. This is where you excel. You can now take your client out of **their** comfort zone and bring them into **your** comfort zone of innate knowledge and ability.

Unearthing Your Purpose

This is an exercise in letting go of your pre-conceptions and listening to your inner voice. You've done it once with the animal totem, so it's easier the second time around. It's about understanding what you are here to achieve. It's like unearthing a lump of gold that is heavily caked in mud and dirt. You have to brush the dirt off to find the gold within.

The key to understanding your Purpose is to step into your **vulnerability**, and to let go of your preconceptions. In doing so you open up, relax, and let go of the 'correct' answer, instead providing an answer that is intuitive.

There are two ways you can unearth your Purpose. The first option is to use this link, justinjgcooper.com/purpose-visualisation to access and purchase the 15-minute Temple Visualisation downloadable audio file and questionnaire, for a small fee.

Alternatively, you can have a go at answering the questions below in the more traditional, rational way.

As you know, I believe the 'new' way – using the visualisation technique – is far more effective than the 'old' way. But I want to give you the choice. So if you do decide to answer these questions in a rational state, here are a few important guidelines:

1. Get away from your normal work environment to somewhere where you can relax, such as a living room or bedroom.

2. Before you start answering the questions, do the same slow, deep breathing exercise that you did during the animal totem visualisation. As a reminder, this involves breathing in through your nose slowly and deeply (into your belly) for a count of five seconds, then breathing out through your nose for another count of five. Repeat this five times and you should start to feel relaxed and ready to answer the questions more intuitively.

3. Take the first answer that comes to your mind – don't reject it because it sounds 'out there' – just write it down. You can make sense of it later.

10. Questions to help uncover your Work Purpose

Here are the work Purpose questions, should you decide not to do the visualisation. Remember that you can answer these questions as an individual, as a business owner, or as a brand custodian.

If you are a brand custodian, the secret is to put yourself inside the brand, by taking on the persona of that brand. Obviously you'll need to use your imagination to answer these questions in terms of a brand, and have fun with this. Have a crack at question 6 – imagine where your brand would want to take its holiday. You can ignore question 10 for obvious reasons.

1. What are you here to do?

_____

_____

2. What do you love most about life?

_____

_____

3. What do you stand for?

_____

_____

4. What do you stand against?

_____

_____

5. What are you really passionate about?

_____

_____

6. If you didn't have to work, what would you choose to do?

_____

_____

7. What aspects of your work (current and past) have inspired you the most?

_____

_____

8. What aspects of your work (current and past) give you the biggest sense of satisfaction?

_____

_____

9. What aspects of your work (current and past) make you feel most valued?

_____

_____

10. If you were told you only had a week to live, what's the one thing you would regret not having done in your life?

_____

_____

As you'll see, there are questions about what you want, alongside questions about what you don't want. This is important, because it's often the shadow that gives us inspiration. By 'the shadow' I'm referring to the negative stuff you are struggling with and/or what you stand against. Don't be tempted to ignore this; it's a great source of inspiration to explain what you are here to solve in the world. And it can become the basis of how you communicate to your audience – by naming the problem you have faced and overcome.

Knowing that you are here to fix a major headache they've been struggling with themselves is an excellent way to make a deep connection with your tribe.

What to do with your Purpose answers?

Whether you have used the Purpose visualisation to answer these questions or you have just answered the questions above, you can now write a simple Purpose statement, using the pro forma on the next page.

I / We / my brand believe(s)...

- Insert a statement using some or all of the answers to questions 3, 4 & 5.

Example: I believe the key to discovering your uniqueness is to unlock your *Purpose*.

_____

_____

_____

When you understand the Purpose behind your work, you shift your thinking from *what* you do, to *why* you do it. This gives you greater clarity on who you are, and what you are here to do.

I am / we are / my brand is here to….

- Insert a statement using some or all of your answers to questions 1, 2, 6, 7, 8 & 9.

Example: I am here to inspire people to discover their true selves – so they can ignore what others tell them and discover their authentic uniqueness. I am here to help people, businesses and brands to make a deeper connection with their tribes.

_____

_____

_____

You will notice that I left out question 10 from this exercise. Question 10 is about remembering what you really want from life, so it may be personal rather than business related. If, however, there is a connection to the work you do, you can use your answer to bring greater passion and clarity to either your 'believe' statement or your 'here to...' wording.

Internal v. external drivers

The two exercises you have done so far, **animal totem** and **Purpose,** explain your internal drivers. This is what's important to you, your business, or your brand. They are internal drivers that explain why you feel driven to do the work you do.

Now we're going to translate that internal drive and take it externally, to explain what your **Mission** is, and to understand how this enriches the lives of your **ideal clients**.

In other words, Purpose is your internal guide, while Mission is your external objective.

Defining Your Mission

If Purpose answers the question 'Why am I here?' Mission answers the question 'What are you here to do for people?'

This is about understanding what you are here to change or challenge. Now some of what you've worked on in the Purpose area spills over, but here the focus is not on what's important to you but what's important to them. And of course there should be a direct link between what you want to do for yourself and how this changes or improves the situation for your clients.

As before, you have two options – you can either do this using the visualisation I have created to help you access your subconscious, or you can answer some questions rationally.

The Mission visualisation is different from the 'animal totem' and 'Purpose' visualisations because it uses a variation of an NLP technique called 'timeline therapy' (which has been around for about 30 years). This involves imagining that you can go forward in time to a point where you have already achieved success, whatever your concept of success involves. It is a very powerful exercise because it fires up the imagination to a world of possibilities, asking the question 'what if...?'

Here's the link:
justinjgcooper.com/mission-visualisation
to purchase and download the 20-minute audio recording and accompanying questionnaire, for a small fee.

If you don't want to do the visualisation, here are the questions that you can ask yourself 'rationally.' Just be aware that this excludes the 'dream of your ideal future' part of the visualisation, and that the ideas you come up with from a rational standpoint are likely to be far less powerful than the ideas you develop when you access them through your subconscious.

Again, if you are managing a brand, imagine that you have adopted the character and personality of that brand. Use your imagination to answer these questions in terms of a brand. And yes, you can ignore question 10 – because brands are designed to be immortal!

10 Questions to Help Uncover Your Work Mission

1. How do you want to change the lives of your clients/customers?

_____

_____

2. What problem were you/your business/your brand born to solve for your audience?

_____

_____

3. How will you make a difference to the people you serve?

_____

_____

4. How will you change the market you work in/are looking at working in?

(Think in terms of overturning an injustice, or solving a major problem that currently exits, or changing the rules)

_____

_____

5. What is the biggest positive impact of your work/business/brand?

_____

_____

6. What are the main outcomes that your work/business/brand delivers?

_____

_____

7. What legacy do you want to leave to the world?

_____

_____

8. What big idea do you have to 'change the game?'

_____

_____

9. Why is it so important that you do this work, or offer this product or service?

_____

_____

10. If you were told you only had a week to live, what's the one thing you would regret not having given to in the world?

_____ _____

_____

What to do with your Mission answers

After answering these questions (using the 'new' or 'old' way), you can now write a simple Mission statement, using this pro forma:

My / Our Mission is to...

- Insert a statement using some or all of the answers to questions 1, 2, 7 & 8.

Example: My Mission is to unlock your Purpose and discover the secret recipe behind what makes you unique.

_____

_____

_____

I am/we are doing this in order to….

- Insert a statement using some or all of the answers to questions 3, 4, 5, 6 & 9.

Example: I am doing this in order to show people how to build their careers, businesses, and/or brands 'on Purpose' – so they are more motivated, more connected, and more successful.

_____

_____

_____

Again I have left out question 10 from the pro forma for the same reason that it may be more personal rather than business related. If you can see a connection to the work you do or the product or service you offer, you can add it to either statement.

Defining Your Ideal Client

The final step is to get clear on who you're here to help. Note I'm avoiding using the term 'target market,' because I believe the *intention* behind that term is wrong. For me this smacks of painting a target on the victim, then gunning him or her down. However, the term 'ideal client' is much more akin to the concept of *purposing*, because it describes the person you are here to help. It defines who your Mission was created for.

Armed with this last piece of information, we can now join up the dots between:

1. Who you really are (animal totem)

2. Why you're here (Purpose)

3. What you're here to do, and

4. Who you're here to do it for.

And yes of course there **is** a visualisation for this…

Click on this link:
justinjgcooper.com/ideal-client-visualisation to purchase and download the audio recording and questionnaire for a small fee.

As before, you have the option to choose to answer the following questions rationally instead, but the visualisation has much more to it, and is likely to take you a lot further. But if you'd prefer not to choose the visualisation, there are 10 questions to consider listed below.

Once again, if you are managing a brand, use your imagination to answer these questions on behalf of the brand, having fun with the experience.

10 Questions to help uncover your ideal client.

1. Describe the person/the people who you believe are most likely to need your help.

Please describe them in terms of gender, age, the work they do, where they live, etc.

_____

_____

_____

2. What is the biggest problem that they are struggling with, that you/your business/your brand was made to solve?

_____

_____

3. What do they need most from you right now?

_____

_____

4. How will you change their thinking?

_____

_____

5. How will you improve their lives?

_____

_____

6. What unique gifts do you have that help solve their problems?

_____

_____

7. What other talents, skills, or abilities do you bring that will make a difference to them?

_____

_____

8. What benefits and/or outcomes do you provide them with?

_____

_____

9. Why have they chosen you/your business/your brand instead of anyone else?

_____

_____

10. How do you feel now you have 'met' this person?

_____

_____

What to do with your ideal client answers

Write a simple description of your ideal client, using this pro forma:

This is the person/these are the people I am here to help:

- Insert your answer to questions 1.

_____

_____

This is the problem they have that I was born to solve:

- Insert a summary of your answers to questions 2 & 3.

_____

_____

_____

This how I make a difference to them:

- Insert a summary of your answers to question 4, 5, 6, 7, & 8.

_____

_____

_____

This is why my ideal client chooses me/my business/my brand instead of anyone else:

- Insert your answer to question 9.

_____

_____

_____

Question 10 is thrown in there to remind you of how great it is to finally 'meet' the person you are here to help. Use your answer to inspire you to go and find them, and to remind yourself that they need you as much as you need them.

So there you have it – you've completed the dots.

You now have a series of words and/or statements that define why you're here, what you're here to do and who you are here to do it for. This is your _purposing_ statement.

Now it's time to activate your Purpose and _unleash your beast_.

Chapter 9
Unleash Your Beast

Now you have your *purposing statement*, it's time to unleash your beast.

And that means creating a Vision for how you will achieve it.

To do this we'll need to fire up your imagination.

The power of Imagination

Edward de Bono wrote that creativity and innovation are not linear; they happen in leaps and bounds. Far from being a rational process – as the 'Gang of Three' Greek philosophers would have us believe – de Bono stated that it is only with hindsight that we construct a more logical and linear explanation for how we got from 'no idea' to 'brilliant idea.'

Pure creativity seems to come to us at the speed of light. That's because it doesn't operate at a logical, step-by-step pace. It rushes in, all of a sudden. That's the power of imagination. It only comes to us when we let go of logical, rational thought, and that means suspending our belief in what we know (our reality) for a while. Intuitive thought is fast and radical, while rational thinking is slower and more 'expected.'

For you to 'unleash your beast' and start the process of creating your ideal career, business, or brand, you first need to imagine what it will look like. You need to create a Vision for it. If you did the Mission Visualisation earlier, then you will be familiar with this technique.

If you didn't, then it's important to focus on these three words: '**Just let go**.' In doing so, you ignore your current constraints and switch off your critical, rational mind. This is quite hard to do for most people – in the Western world at least – thanks to a schooling system that tends to focus on developing rational thought. But as creativity comes from your imagination, it's important to set your intention to thinking differently.

The secret behind any brilliant idea is to imagine what **could** be, and ignore the facts of what currently is. This is the leap of faith needed to let go of one reality and replace it with a new (and hopefully better) one.

And for this to happen, you need to learn to fly.

Learning to Fly

According to *The Hitchhikers Guide to The Galaxy*, (by Douglas Adams) the trick to learning to fly is "to aim at the ground and miss." In the book, Ford Prefect (an alien from the planet Betelgeuse Seven) is explaining the process to the last remaining earthling, Arthur Dent.

Ford says "you've just gotta ignore the ground." Arthur replies, "how the hell am I supposed to do that? It's hard and it's coming up against me pretty fast!"

Then Ford reveals the secret: "You have to fall and then at the last minute when you're gonna hit the ground you have to focus on something else, you have to distract your mind and then you'll find yourself floating, hovering and once you're hovering you can start to soar, to fly and pick back off the ground."

This is what Arthur learns to do. Sure, he hits the ground a few times when he forgets that he's flying and that flying is actually impossible. But with practice he masters the technique.

The trick to creating a Vision for where you want your career, business, and/or brand to go, is exactly the same as learning to fly. You have to:

1. **Fall:** Let go of the reality of your current situation and suspend disbelief.

2. **Distract:** Switch off your rational mind through relaxing, exercising, meditating – or by using any other mindfulness technique that closes down that

part of your brain that screams 'You're not good enough to be *that* successful!'

3. **Fly:** Let your imagination soar by imagining that *anything* is possible.

Harnessing the power of your imagination is about forgetting the ground is there and flying.

If you still have reservations about the benefits of dreaming of a better future, here's what Albert Einstein said:

"Everything is energy and that's all there is to it. Match the frequency of the reality you want and you cannot help but get that reality. It can be no other way. This is not philosophy. This is physics."

What Albert is referring to here is Quantum Physics, and the discovery that when you focus on an objective, you literally send energy towards that objective to help make it happen. The ancient mystics referred to this as 'The Law of Attraction.' Western science is now catching up with what the Eastern shamans have known for thousands of years.

Your final exercise

So for this final exercise I want you to imagine what ultimate success means to you. If you are managing a brand, this exercise is for you personally to see where you imagine your work taking you in the future.

Regardless of whether you are in a career, running or managing a business, or managing a brand, I want you to think big. Don't short-change yourself on your Vision – go ahead and flex that creative, imaginative mind of yours!

There's only one way to go to unearth your Vision. I'd love to offer you a set of questions to answer, but I just don't know how to do this exercise using rational questioning. So I can only offer you access using this link:
justinjgcooper.com/vision-visualisation
to purchase the Vision Visualisation downloadable audio file and questionnaire, for a small fee. It will give you a framework to create a Vision for your future. It's designed to engage your intuitive brain so you can create a thumbnail sketch of what you want to create in the future. You'll hear my voice taking you on a journey, accompanied by relaxing music.

Once you've finished this exercise, turn over and answer the questions on the next page. But please **don't turn over and read these questions yet** – as this may allow your rational mind to influence the intuitive answers that the meditation is designed to elicit. Good luck and enjoy, and I'll see you on the other side of this exercise...

Vision Visualisation Questions

1. How did you imagine your future – what was it like?

_____

_____

_____

_____

2. Where did you imagine that you would be living and working?

_____

_____

_____

_____

3. What was your role and/or job title in this future time?

_____

_____

4. What did you imagine that you had already achieved in the future time?

_____

_____

5. What did you imagine having in the future that you don't have right now?

_____

_____

6. What was your future self like – physically, mentally, and emotionally?

_____

_____

7. What's the biggest difference between your future life and your life now?

_____

_____

8. What are the most exciting things about the future you imagined?

_____

_____

9. If your Vision came true, what's the biggest positive impact you could make to the world?

_____

_____

10. What advice did your future self give you?

_____

_____

11. How do you feel after doing this exercise?

_____

_____

12. What action could you to take **now** to move you towards your Vision?

_____

_____

Planning your Vision

Now you've completed the exercise, we're going to use a rational thought process to map out a potential roadmap to achieving your Vision. This needs to be loose and flexible, because you never know what random opportunities will show up to help you achieve your Vision faster and more efficiently than your rational mind can predict.

Step 1

Build up your Vision in terms of location, scale and scope

For this Vision to happen...

1A. Where will you be based?

_____

1B. What is the scope of your new role/career, or what will your business/brand be doing to change the market it operates in?

_____

_____

1C. How will you change the rules within your area/market?

_____

_____

1D. How will you make a real difference to your customers?

_____

_____

1E. How will you do things differently to others?

_____

_____

1F. What will you be earning, or what revenue will your business/brand be generating (ballpark only)?

_____

_____

Step 2

How do your answers above compare with the answers you gave in Chapter 8?

– How do they relate to and support your Purpose?

If the link is not obvious, think outside the box to see the broader connection.

_____

_____

_____

– How do they support or expand your Mission?

_____

_____

_____

− How do they relate to the ideal client you identified?

_____

_____

_____

Step 3

Where are you now?

Answer questions 1A to 1H in terms of your current situation:

3A. Where are you currently based?

_____

3B. What is the scope of your current role/career, or your business/brand?

_____

_____

3C. How do you currently challenge the rules within your area/market?

_____

_____

_____

3D. How do you make a real difference to your customers?

_____

_____

_____

3E. How do you do things differently to others?

_____

_____

_____

3F. What do you earn, or what revenue does your business/brand generate?

_____

Step 4

What has to change?

4A. What are the three biggest differences between your life in Step 1 to Step 3?

_____

_____

_____

_____

4B. In a simple sentence explain in broad terms, what key changes have to take place for you to achieve your Vision?

_____

_____

_____

_____

Step 5

How do you feel about this change?

5A. How will you feel when you have achieved it?

_____

_____

_____

5B. What are the benefits of this change?

_____

_____

_____

5C. What are the drawbacks?

_____

_____

_____

Step 6

What are the barriers?

What are the five main existing barriers preventing you from achieving your Vision?

- Think about this from an internal (your mindset) and external (market factors) point of view

Barrier 1:

_____

_____

Barrier 2:

_____

_____

Barrier 3:

_____

_____

Step 7

What can you do to overcome these barriers?

How will you have to change your way of thinking?

Who do you know who could help you overcome these barriers?

Solution 1:

_____

_____

Solution 2:

_____

_____

Solution 3:

_____

_____

Step 8

Who do you know who could help you achieve this Vision?

Think of family, friends, and/or associates who work (or know someone who does work) in the field or area you imagined working in. Write a list of who they are and how they could help you achieve your Vision.

_____

_____

_____

Step 9

Create three steps to show how you might move from your current situation to your Vision. Create each step as an achievable stretch goal, even though you don't have the resources or contacts right now to achieve it. These resources will come with intention and planning. These may well show up as you start to discuss this with your family, friends, and contacts.

Tips:

a) Use the section below to draft your steps. Do this exercise in pencil initially, so you can modify your steps after your initial draft.

b) Work backwards from the Vision, starting with Step 3, describing the situation you will be in at that point. Then work back to Step 2, again describing the situation you see yourself in at that point. Lastly describe your situation in Step 1.

c) Having drafted your steps, you may find that you want to step up the goals in one stage, or perhaps ease off a little, so that the move from one step to the next is more evenly weighted.

In reality, you are highly unlikely to move through these exact steps. However this exercise is really important, as it helps your rational mind picture how, in theory, it could be possible to move from your current situation to the Vision your imagination created.

Step 1

_____

_____

Step 2

_____

_____

Step 3

_____

_____

What next?

Start day-dreaming – it's good for you. The more you practice using your intuition, the better you'll get at discovering useful and hidden information about yourself, how you do your best work, and how you can make a difference in your field. Intuitive thinking also prompts further leaps of imagination.

Get excited by the idea – use your emotional brain to imagine how you'll feel once you reach your goal. Tap into this excitement on a regular basis, so you don't allow your rational mind to kill the idea before it's had a chance to get going.

Bring your Idea to life visually and audibly – create a 'mood board' for your Vision using images and words you find on the web, which you can cut and paste onto a document and print out to pin up on a wall at home and/or in your work space. Here's my own 'mood board' that I created in 2015 to picture the experience I wanted to give my clients when they worked with me:

You can also add music for fun - creating a 'brand track' to inspire and lift you whenever the task seems hard.

Share your idea – the more you discuss your idea with your trusted entourage, the more 'legs' it has. This is also where the rational and practical aspects kick in to help you stress test the details of your idea, and make improvements to your Vision along the way.

As my friend Carole Issa from Alephpreneur said:

"Good execution starts by sharing your idea. It'll allows you to stress test every aspect of it."

When you are explaining your idea, use an analogy to give the listener a frame of reference for how the idea would work. For instance, if you were designing a jetpack that used a solar propulsion system, you could start by telling the story of Icarus, the mythical Greek character, who flew too close to the sun and who fell from the sky. Of course you'd assure your potential customers that your jet pack will have no such limitations! The association you create between your idea and a well-known story or anecdote anchors the idea in your audience's mind. If a picture can tell a 1,000 words, an analogy can tell 100,000 words.

And finally – do a reality check.

Who are the main players in the market today and what do they offer? What are the main customer groups, and what are they looking for? How does your idea create its own niche, while meeting the needs of a group of consumers that you can nurture into your tribe? How could your idea be adapted and/or improved in terms of its design, features, and benefits to be even more appealing?

By following these key steps you'll be using all parts of your brain to achieve your Vision: your intuitive (reptilian) brain, your emotional (limbic) brain, and your rational brain (frontal lobes). As we'll see in the next and final chapter, this is the key to developing a really smart idea that stands the test of time.

Chapter 10
Change the World

Welcome to the final chapter of this book. Hopefully you'll agree we have been on quite a journey together since we started out in Chapter 1.

If I have done my job properly, you should now have a fairly good handle on:

1. Why **authenticity** is such an important part of the buying process today, and how explaining *why*

you do what you do is crucial to engendering trust in your prospects, prospective employers, customers, business partners, employees, and subcontractors.

2. Why it's so important to **start with you** when planning and developing your career, product, or service. You will know that I believe that defining your Purpose is the single most important factor in establishing a successful career, business, or brand, and that it's very hard to define that Purpose when you are in a rational state of mind.

3. The reality that **you can't expect your customers to tell you what to do** for them, because they don't know what you are capable of, or what amazing ideas you have for them.

4. The fact that it's a good idea to **ignore your competitors** when you are looking for your unique offer, because they have their own Purpose and unique capabilities, which are different from yours.

5. The **benefits of being 'on Purpose'** – clarity of Vision, motivation, ease of decision-making, improved leadership skills, unifying affects behind a common goal, engendering of trust, ease of

recruitment, and the definition of uniqueness that it brings.

6. The difference between *purposing* and 'traditional marketing'; with the former being about putting **you** front and centre of the equation, defining your Purpose and delivering it via a Mission to help like-minded customers overcome the problem you are here to solve for them.

7. The benefits of launching new products, services, and careers based on your **'why foundation'**, ensuring everything you offer aligns not only with your own beliefs and values, but also with those of your tribe.

8. The **four key steps to *purposing***: unearthing the real you, defining your Purpose, defining your Mission, and defining your ideal client.

9. The **benefits of total intelligence or TI** – combining rational, emotional and intuitive thinking to deliver a higher level of intelligence, in order to build your business, brand, and/or career in a smarter way.

10. The need to **take off the mask** to discover the real person you were born to be, or genuine culture you are here to create, and to strip away

any negative conditioning by family, friends, managers, and co-workers that say we're not good enough as we are.

11. How to use the **visualisations and intuitive questions** to discover and define:

- What you, your business, and/or your brand stand for,

- Your Purpose and your Mission,

- The ideal client that you are here to serve

- What you offer that's truly unique.

12. How to let go and fly with your ideas and dreams.

13. What your Vision for the future looks like; where the work you do is inspirational to you and others, and how to get from where you are now to where you want to be.

I don't know about you, but it's been quite a journey. It's taken me four years to get this book to you, and I hope you have enjoyed it. It's been like a silent scream keeping this information to myself for so long, but now it's out in the open. I hope it will create more discussion and further development in the field of business mindfulness.

But before we call it a day, we have one small thing left to do: change the world.

While the idea of 'changing the world' might sound like a stretch, remember that the notion of 'just doing your thing' and 'not trying to be too different' are just throwbacks to Industrial Revolution thinking – where we needed to be good, compliant cogs in the big wheel of industry. But in the new 'conscious' world of business, we are being asked to be more creative, original, and to make a difference.

So there isn't actually a huge gap between 'changing the world' and having the belief that you can make a difference with the work you do. It's just a matter of magnitude.

Why do I even ask you to think in terms of 'changing the world?'

The answer is that by setting your intentions on something big, your Vision will be that much more inspiring for you, and the people you need to bring along with you on your journey (customers, business partners, and so on). Martin Luther King set the bench pretty high when he shared his dream that one day his black son would be treated as an equal in a white society.

Given that his speech was made in 1963, at a time when race relations were at a boiling point in the US, you can see how this really was a 'change the world' statement. Why didn't he aim a little lower? What didn't he start with say a target of securing equal pay for all workers, regardless of colour? Or to work on abolishing segregation in the US? He aimed for something much bigger in order to motivate and inspire people with a dream of what could be.

And that's what I want you to do: review your Vision and dial it up, so it really is a 'change the world' idea. Focus on Question 9 of the movie visualisation, which relates to what you will be doing for people in the future. Take it from the notion of 'helping them' to 'changing their world.' Make it as big as Martin Luther King's statement. Then look at how it could impact your Vision. Do you need to amend your Vision now? Does it now go further than you originally thought? Do you need to modify the three steps you need to get there?

Remember that the greater your belief and intention, the greater the impact. We all have far more potential within us than we realise, but we 'keep ourselves small' in order not to stand out too much. Well guess what? The time to 'stand out' is now! There's no point in having a gift if you don't use it, and it doesn't work unless you activate it.

The ultimate outcome of being 'on Purpose' is to change the world, because once you are clear on what you are here to achieve, the game changes. Your focus switches from thinking in terms of what you can **get**, to how you can **help.** This is at the heart of *Purposing* - delivering your secret ingredient to a like-minded audience, so you can change the world. And this mindset, that nothing can stop you from changing the world, is a crucial final step in this book. Because all the wonderful things you've discovered here about yourself, your work, your business, and your brand **must** be put to good use. Armed with your Purpose, Mission and Vision, changing the world should be an absolute breeze!

And should the echo of my voice from this book start to fade, and you feel your confidence waning, just remember this...

The world *has* changed, and the desire for authenticity and genuineness is only going to increase. Your role is to simply be yourself and use your raw natural talent and unique gift to help others. Do *that* and you can't help but make a difference. Dial it up to the next level and you can't help but change the world.

And if you do nothing else after reading this book, please:

'Be yourself, because everyone else is already taken.'

Dedications

To Lynne – thank you for your immense patience and love as I worked out how to be on Purpose while still being able to put food on the table at the same time. You rock.

To Katie and Tasha - you are the best things I ever helped create in my life. You *are* my rock.

To Mum – I love you more than I can ever say. We all do.

To Nick and Chris – never were three brothers closer.

To Dad – I miss you. You really should have written that children's book before you "shuffled off this mortal coil." This is for you.

About

Justin JG Cooper is a hopeless optimist. He actually believes that we have a chance of saving this planet from greed, war, and environmental destruction. Ridiculous of course, but he keeps on dreaming.

The basis of this wild dream is that humans are now learning to think differently. In particular, they are learning to trust and use their intuition again, and to combine this with emotional and rational intelligence. The outcome is a new level of intelligence he calls TI, which stands for Total Intelligence.

In some small way, Justin hopes this book will add to the new level of thinking that is slowly expanding across the globe.

72125644R00103

Made in the USA
Columbia, SC
13 June 2017